THE
ENGLISH HERITAGE
DIRECTORY OF
BUILDING LIMES

THE
ENGLISH HERITAGE
DIRECTORY OF
BUILDING LIMES

Manufacturers and Suppliers of
Building Limes in the United Kingdom
and the Republic of Ireland

DONHEAD

Editor: Jeanne Marie Teutonico
Consultant Editor: Kit Wedd

First published in the United Kingdom 1997 by
Donhead Publishing Ltd
Lower Coombe
Donhead St Mary
Shaftesbury
Dorset SP7 9LY

ISBN 1-873394-21-7

Designed by Paul Sands
Printed by: The Cromwell Press Ltd

Commercial disclaimer
The many companies and specialist groups referred to, and/or advertising, in this
directory have been listed and invited to contribute on the basis of their
involvement in the field of building conservation and/or the suitability of some of
their products and services for works to historic buildings and ancient monuments.
Some of these companies and individuals also supply products and services to
other areas of the building market which have little or no application in the building
conservation field. The inclusion of any company, group or individual in this
publication should not be regarded as either a recommendation or endorsement
by English Heritage or by its agents.

Accuracy of Information
The information contained in this publication is only as accurate as the entries
provided and/or confirmed by those listed. Whilst every effort has been made to
ensure faithful reproduction of the original or amended text, the editor, publisher
and English Heritage can accept no responsibility for the data produced in or
omitted from this publication. The contribution of entries and amendments for the
next edition is welcomed.

Definitions
No legal implication is given by the use of the terms agent, owner or operator
within this directory. As we go to press some lime kilns and factories are changing
hands, and operating licences are renegotiated from time to time.

Front cover
Lime slaking at Lulworth Castle. Photo: English Heritage/Iain McCaig

Contents

Foreword   vi

Acknowledgements   viii

Introduction   ix

Chapter 1

Classification of Building Limes and Related Products   1

Chapter 2

Alphabetical Directory of Producers and Suppliers   11

Chapter 3

Glossary   42

Chapter 4

Bibliography and Standards   47

Chapter 5

Suppliers by Region and Product Finder   51

Reply form   59

Foreword

I am pleased to introduce readers to the first edition of *The English Heritage Directory of Building Limes.* The directory has grown out of a series of technical and scientific studies on lime and lime-based materials which forms part of our strategic research programme in the cathedral grants scheme. The research is focused on understanding historic building material decay problems commonly found in the English cathedrals, and on formulating practical, benign and cost-effective treatments which are relevant to a much larger section of the country's historic property.

English Heritage and its predecessor organisations responsible for the maintenance and repair of nationally important ancient monuments have been constant users of lime in all its forms for most of this century. As early as 1913, the Ministry of Works Chief Architect Frank Baines commented that 'the deleterious effect of Portland cement on (historic) stonework is becoming more widely known' and set out standards of practice in the use of lime in *General Instructions to Foremen in Charge of the Works of Preservation,* an appendix to the Report of the Chief Inspector for Ancient Monuments and Historic Buildings in that year.

The present resurgence of interest in the properties and usefulness of building limes is to be applauded and encouraged, as far as building conservation is concerned. Architects and building surveyors who specialise in the repair and maintenance of historic buildings have always specified lime-based materials. Many country builders and masons continue to follow the lime tradition without question, as their forefathers did. But now, as the scale of building refurbishment increases and the care of older property is shared with more general practitioners, the wider building industry is also adopting lime for mortars, plasters, renders and grouts.

Here I must acknowledge the pioneering work of the Society for the Protection of Ancient Buildings and its volunteer members in promoting the use of this essential raw material. Similar advocacy is provided by the postgraduate building conservation courses and by influential authors, so that there should now be few in the conservation world who have not heard of lime-based materials and their special suitability for conservation work. Interested practitioners, researchers, manufacturers and educators have also recently formed an association, The Building Limes Forum – with a regular journal, site visits and meetings – to study and promote the material in more depth.

But there is still much work to be done, and here I offer a word of caution. It should be remembered that Ordinary Portland cement's widespread conquest of the building industry was not an accidental process. The de-skilling of the Victorian building industry and the loss of knowledge about traditional practice in the use of lime in an age of great change naturally led to the wholesale adoption of the product that was standardised, mass produced and of known composition and performance, and which therefore required very little in the way of site preparation and use. This trend intensified after each World War as standards of craftsmanship continued to wane. Now we risk another reaction against the resurgent use of lime, if well-meaning but inexperienced practitioners misuse the material through a lack of basic guidance.

This is not to say, of course, that cement is always bad and lime is always good: there are circumstances where both materials have a role to play in conservation and we must understand their potential and limitations if standards of practice are to rise. But now that we are experiencing a revival in the use of lime, when there are more novices amongst user groups than ever before, it is important to realise that 'lime' is a generic term for a large range of materials which possess subtly different chemical and mineralogical constituents, and differ in modes of manufacture, preparation and application to vary the quality and performance of the final product, be it a mortar, plaster, render, grout or limewash.

Although there is now a wide range of standard and bespoke, traditionally-processed lime products on the market, not all manufacturers are able to provide customers with technical support. The specifier and the practitioner must make every effort to ascertain the origin, properties and consistency of the materials in question and to determine their suitability for the intended purpose.

All of this is difficult for the building industry because of ignorance concerning published standards for non-hydraulic limes and the complete lack of a British standard, or of an agreed European standard, for hydraulic limes – which creates confusion regarding the typologies and qualities of the materials appropriate for inclusion in specifications.

Inevitably, this directory cannot offer guidance on specification or on issues of quality control. The bibliography cites relevant sources of further information, and English Heritage's technical policies and advice on appropriate conservation recipes and practice remain constant, as referred to in our *Practical Building Conservation Technical Handbooks* and *The Repair of Historic Buildings*.

I hope that this simple directory will contribute to the better understanding and use of building limes, and will help to foster the development of a revitalised lime industry.

John Fidler RIBA
Head of Architectural Conservation
Department of Conservation
English Heritage

Acknowledgements

Many individuals have contributed to the production of this directory. In particular, acknowledgements and thanks are due to Historic Building and Site Services, Bournemouth University, for producing the original draft of this directory under contract to English Heritage; to Jeanne Marie Teutonico and Sasha Barnes of the Architectural Conservation team at English Heritage, who revised and updated the text; to Michael Wingate, for his invaluable comments on the technical content; to Kit Wedd, our consultant editor, who gave coherence and structure to the book whilst gently pushing us to complete our tasks; and finally to Donhead Publishing for its guidance and patient attention to detail during the publication process.

Introduction

The use of traditional materials in the repair and maintenance of historic buildings and ancient monuments has long been accepted practice in the United Kingdom. Provided they are correctly applied, traditional materials offer long-term benefits in building conservation that cannot be matched by modern and potentially damaging substitutes. In general, traditional materials tend to be similar to original historic fabric in properties such as porosity, strength and appearance; and such factors are extremely important to successful conservation work.

Consequently, there is a renewed demand for 'authentic' materials that are compatible with old buildings. In response, a great variety of large and small producers, suppliers, educators, advisory services and associated heritage organisations have been conducting research and developing products, facilities and information to serve the building trade in general, and those engaged in conservation in particular.

Lime is one of the traditional building materials which has experienced something of a renaissance in the last 20 years. It is one of the most important and versatile of materials available to the building trade and is essential to the production of traditional mortars, external renders, plasters, limewashes and other finishes.

Traditional mortars and renders that are rich in lime are inherently permeable and therefore allow moisture to evaporate with ease. Cement-rich mortars are by contrast dense and impermeable; they block the natural 'breathing' qualities of historic masonry walls and renders, causing moisture to be retained and, potentially, to damage fragile brick, stone and earth walls. Furthermore, lime-based products are relatively low in strength and are flexible, with a natural elasticity that allows them to expand and contract to accommodate structural settlement and thermal movement. Cement-based substitutes, on the other hand, are strong and rigid and will not 'give' with a building as it moves, thus creating stresses that can damage adjacent historic masonry.

For these and other reasons, it is generally recommended that the repair and maintenance of old mortars, renders, plasters and finishes should involve the use of lime-based materials. There are, of course, some situations where the use of lime is incorrect or inadvisable, but these will be the exceptions in the context of historic buildings. It is therefore extremely important that lime-based materials are well understood, easily acquired, and properly applied.

Fortunately, manufacturers and suppliers throughout the UK are providing a wide range of lime-based products and related materials and services which are available to institutions, businesses and individual owners of historic properties. Many firms will respond to individual requirements for a particular colour or mix of materials for a specified render or mortar. Some firms also provide technical advisory services and information on how to apply their materials.

The English Heritage Directory of Building Limes is intended to encourage and facilitate the use of lime in the building industry by providing a comprehensive list of producers and suppliers of lime-based materials in the United Kingdom and the Republic of Ireland. For the purposes of this directory, the term 'lime-based materials' has been understood to mean both non-hydraulic and hydraulic limes as well as pre-mixed mortars, limewashes and related materials.

A general discussion of the types and classification of building limes and related products is given in the following section. This information is intended to provide a framework for the directory of products which follows but does not constitute a guideline for the use of lime-based products. Sources of more detailed information on the characteristics and correct use of lime-based building materials are listed in Chapter 4: Bibliography and Standards.

In an ever-changing industry, it is difficult to be inclusive and the editors apologise in advance for any omissions in the list of companies and organisations involved in the production and promotion of lime products. A reply form is provided at the end of the directory for those wishing to provide feedback or information for future editions.

Chapter 1

Classification of Building Limes and Related Products

Limestones, including chalk, provide the raw material for the building limes of the British Isles. In other countries, materials such as marble, sea shells, coral, or other naturally occurring forms of calcium carbonate are used as additional or alternative sources. In the UK and Ireland, however, the only current source of building limes is limestone.

Limestone is a general term for all sedimentary rocks whose principal constituent is calcium carbonate. Within the UK, limestones are obtained from a number of geological formations which were last extensively classified in relation to lime manufacture by the then Building Research Station (Department of Scientific and Industrial Research) in the 1920s. As each formation has particular characteristics, the quality and chemical properties of UK limestones vary considerably. Their composition and characteristics will influence the type of lime produced, its production process and the purposes for which the particular lime will be used. A common classification of the different types of building limes is given in the table on p.10

Non-hydraulic limes

Definition

Non-hydraulic limes, also known as 'air limes', are so called because they will not set chemically under water but require exposure to carbon dioxide in air in order to harden. Such limes are produced from limestones which are relatively pure sources of calcium carbonate ($CaCO_3$) but which may contain varying amounts of magnesium carbonate ($MgCO_3$), the latter ranging up to 45% in what are known as magnesian limestones or dolomites.

Classification of Non-hydraulic limes

Non-hydraulic limes are broadly classified by their chemical content and by their purity. In general, a distinction can be drawn between *calcium limes,* which contain 85% or more of calcium oxide and *magnesian limes,* which contain over 10 to 20% (or more) of magnesium oxide.

Both calcium and magnesian limes are suitable for building and, historically, choice depended on local geology. At present, however, all of the non-hydraulic building limes produced and supplied in the UK and Ireland are calcium limes.

As regards purity, the common classification is as follows:

Fat limes (also known as rich, white, pure or high-calcium limes) contain 5% or less of impurities such as clay (silica and alumina). Such limes slake rapidly, producing much heat, and double or more in volume during the process. They have a high degree of plasticity and are usually white in colour.

Lean limes, also known as poor limes, contain more than 5% of impurities and are therefore less pure than fat limes. Lean limes slake more slowly than fat limes, with a smaller increase in volume. They are less plastic than fat limes and can be white or off-white in colour.

Regardless of their purity, all non-hydraulic limes will harden only by slow reaction with carbon dioxide in the air, a process known as carbonation.

Production of non-hydraulic lime

Burning

The first step in the production of non-hydraulic lime is to break the limestone into lumps and heat the raw material in a kiln. Early kilns were sometimes no more than simple clamps of alternate layers of stone and fuel, covered with clay and ventilated through stoke holes. Traditional kilns, however, are normally flare kilns, in which intermittent burning takes place, or draw kilns, in which loading and burning are continuous. Modern rotary kilns are fuelled by coal dust, oil or gas, burning the limestone at temperatures between 900°C and 1200°C. The minimum effective temperature for burning limestone for lime is 880°C, but for this temperature to be reached in the centre of the stone lumps, an overall temperature at the surface of 1000°C is usually necessary.

During burning, carbon dioxide (and any water) is driven off from the calcium carbonate, resulting in the production of calcium (and sometimes magnesium) oxides. This intermediate product is variously known as 'quicklime', 'lump lime' or simply 'unslaked lime'.

Slaking

The next step in the production of non-hydraulic lime is slaking. Slaking is the reaction of the quicklime (calcium and magnesium oxides) with water (H_2O) to produce calcium and magnesium hydroxides. Traditionally, this process was carried out in pits and the slaked lime was left to mature for several months, or even years, gaining in plasticity as it matured. The Roman writer Pliny speaks of ancient Roman laws which dictated that lime was not to be used until it had been slaked for three years. Though such laws may have referred primarily to lime produced for fine plastering, they do attest to ancient knowledge of the advantages to be gained from a long maturing process. These include both increased plasticity as well as the assurance that all of the lime is thoroughly slaked to avoid pitting and popping of the finished mortar or plaster.

If slaking is to be carried out on site, the quicklime delivered should be as fresh as possible and stored in a dry place in airtight bins or in sealed plastic sacks (to avoid air slaking due to contact with moisture and carbon dioxide in the atmosphere which would lead to carbonation).

Slaking on site for repair work is most conveniently carried out in a galvanised steel cold water storage cistern. Clean, potable water is run into the tank to a depth of approximately 300mm (12 inches) and the quicklime is added by shovel. This operation must be carried out slowly and with caution as a violent reaction occurs between the water and the quicklime, often raising the water temperature to boiling point. Eyes must be protected by goggles and exposed skin with gloves and other suitable safety gear. The initial slaking process may be carried out more quickly and safely by first breaking the lumps of quicklime down to a large aggregate size and by using hot water in the tank.

The slaking lime must be hoed and raked and stirred until the visible reaction has ceased. Enough water must be used to prevent the temperature from rising too high, as this would result in the formation of a gritty, crystalline form of calcium hydroxide which would make a very poor slaked lime. However, the addition of too much water ('drowning' the lime) can cause a skin of slaked lime to form around the lumps of quicklime, preventing further hydration. Experience will dictate the correct amount of water required, which can be adjusted as the process demands.

The addition of water and quicklime continues until the desired quantity has been slaked. The resultant milky material should be sieved through a 5mm screen to remove all unburnt lumps and then left to settle overnight. The soft, rather greasy mass of material formed by the settling of the milk of lime is called *lime putty.*

The lime putty, with a shallow covering of water to prevent it from being exposed to carbon dioxide in the air, should be kept for a minimum period of two weeks before use, but two months or longer is a better period if time permits. There is no upper limit to storage if the lime putty has no contact with air; the material only gets better with age. Old, non-hydraulic lime putty which has been covered acquires a consistency like gelatin; it becomes workable and plastic again when beaten ('knocked up') by hand or milled by machine.

Mixing and storage of coarse stuff

In order to achieve a good base for mortar or plaster, it is recommended that the slaked lime putty be mixed with the sand and other aggregates required by the specification and that the constituents be stored together as wet 'coarse stuff' and left for as long as possible to mature. Storage of coarse stuff is best arranged in plastic bins with airtight lids.

The final mixing or 'knocking up' of the coarse stuff must be thorough. This can best be carried out either by using a mortar-mill or by thorough beating and ramming with a simply made wooden rammer or pickaxe handle. In either case, the objectives are to increase the overall lime-aggregate contact and to remove surplus water by compaction of the mass so as to create a highly plastic and workable mortar material.

Hardening of non-hydraulic lime mortars and plasters

The hardening of non-hydraulic lime mortars is due to both evaporation of water and a process known as 'carbonation', the reaction of calcium hydroxide with carbon dioxide in the air forming calcium carbonate. Carbonation is a delicate process which is dependent on many factors including temperature, moisture, the thickness and pore structure of the mortar or plaster and its substrate and, of course, the presence of carbon dioxide.

When coarse stuff is left exposed to air, it stiffens, hardens and shrinks. Lime putty alone undergoes a far greater shrinkage, which is why it is always used with an aggregate, except to butter very fine joints. Only the minimum amount of water (if any) should be added to mature coarse stuff to achieve workability so that changes during drying can be kept to a minimum.

Carbonation will begin while the mortar is still drying out and continue for many years. Rapid drying out, which sometimes takes place in hot or windy weather on unprotected work, seems to retard the carbonation process, resulting in a mortar which is more vulnerable to rain and frost. Care should therefore be taken to keep finished work protected from rain, strong heat and local draughts while encouraging good general air circulation. In certain cases, intermittent mist spraying of the mortar surfaces to prevent rapid drying out and to encourage carbonation may be recommended.

In summary, the hardening of non-hydraulic lime mortars will only take place through contact with air by reaction with atmospheric carbon dioxide ('carbonation') and evaporation of water. This final process completes a sequence of events, usually described as the *lime cycle* (see diagram, p.5), which begins and ends with calcium carbonate.

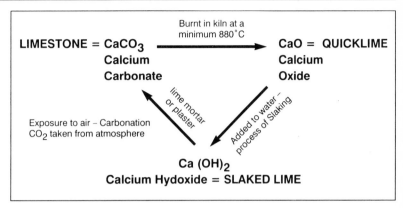

The lime cycle

Forms of non-hydraulic lime

Though some suppliers will still deliver quicklime for slaking on site, most lime is now slaked as part of the production process and sold either as lime putty or as a dry powder known as *hydrated lime* or sometimes simply as *hydrate* or *bag lime*.

The latter dry hydrate is produced at the factory by adding just enough water to the quicklime resulting from burning to satisfy the chemical action of slaking, thus creating a fine slaked powder. Hydrated lime is commonly blended with aggregates in the form of dry, ready-mixed mortars.

Wherever possible, traditionally-made lime putty should be utilised for work on historic buildings due to its superior plasticity and binding properties. If there is no supply available and site slaking is impossible, hydrated lime should be soaked for a minimum of 48 hours in enough clean water to produce a thick cream before use.

Agricultural Lime

Lime and limestones neutralise soil acidity and have been used for centuries for 'liming' fields to improve crop production. The very limited solubility of solid calcium carbonate means that the chalk or other limestone needs to be in powdered form, and the traditional practice was to use lime produced in kilns. The use of burnt lime had the additional advantage of an extremely high alkalinity which made it a more effective acid neutraliser. Today, however, limestone can be crushed and powdered economically and does not require burning. Thus, 'agricultural lime' (pulverised limestone) should not be used as a binder in mortars and renders since unburnt calcium carbonate ($CaCO_3$) will not perform a binding function.

Hydraulic limes

Definition

Hydraulic limes set by chemical reaction with water and so differ from non-hydraulic limes, which harden by reaction with carbon dioxide in the air. Thus hydraulic limes are capable of setting and hardening under water.

The raw material for hydraulic limes is limestone, but limestone which naturally contains a proportion of clay in addition to calcium and magnesium carbonates. Such limestones are known as argillaceous limestones and will yield hydraulic limes of varying characteristics after calcination (burning).

Classification and Standards

Hydraulic limes have traditionally been classified by the amount of active clay materials they contain as indicated below:

Classification	Active clay materials
Feebly hydraulic	<12%
Moderately hydraulic	12% - 18%
Eminently hydraulic	18% - 25%

In general, speed of set in water and ultimate compressive strength achieved will increase with increasingly higher levels of hydraulicity. Thus, a *feebly hydraulic lime* will set more slowly and achieve a lower compressive strength than an eminently hydraulic lime. In addition, it should be noted that some *eminently hydraulic limes* may be pre-gauged at the factory with cement or other hydraulic materials to ensure consistency of hydraulicity; this may lead to variations in composition, colour and salt content that could cause problems when dealing with historic buildings.

There is no British standard for hydraulic limes. In the European Prestandard ENV 459-1: 1995, hydraulic limes produced from argillaceous limestones are designated 'natural hydraulic limes' (NHL), while limes modified by the addition of 'suitable pozzolanic or hydraulic materials, up to 20% by mass' are designated NHL-P.

Production of hydraulic lime

As indicated above, hydraulic limes are produced by burning argillaceous limestones at temperatures somewhat higher than those required for the production of non-hydraulic limes. Kiln temperatures for the production of hydraulic lime can be as high as 1200°C. Kilning procedures are the same as for non-hydraulic lime, but the chemical reactions are much more complex due to the presence of the clayey impurities in the limestone. The burning process produces calcium oxide as well as calcium silicates and calcium aluminates which are responsible for the hydraulic properties of the material. Variations in the raw material as well as in the firing temperature can produce hydraulic limes of very different characteristics.

After burning, the material is subjected to a hydration process. Ideally, this process should just convert the quicklime to powder without causing the calcium silicate components to start to set. In the case of eminently hydraulic limes, the quicklime may need to be subjected to a grinding process prior to hydration.

The resultant product is a hydrated hydraulic lime powder which should be delivered in sealed bags. It is essential that the material be kept sealed and stored in a dry place, as any contact with water or atmospheric moisture can initiate the setting process, causing the binder to lose some or all of its setting properties when used on site.

Mixing and Use

Mixing and use will depend on the type of hydraulic lime. Normally, one part of hydraulic lime is added to either 2.5, 3 or 4 parts aggregate by volume depending on the characteristics required of the mortar. The moderately and eminently hydraulic limes can be mixed with water and aggregates and used immediately like cements. Four hours is a typical time during which such a hydraulic mortar is usable, but eminently hydraulic varieties may have a shorter working period (e.g. two hours) before they begin to set.

In the case of feebly hydraulic limes, the setting process can take much longer. The material should be laid out on a clean board, sprinkled with water, and covered with the required aggregate. It should then be left to stand overnight and knocked up the following morning before use. This overnight standing period in a damp condition ensures that all of the lime is slaked and starts the chemical setting process which is relatively slow in a feebly hydraulic material. The wetting also allows the free lime to fatten up, absorbing water in such a way that it will retain it against the suction of a masonry substrate.

Under no circumstances should any hydraulic mortar be knocked up again and re-used after it has begun to stiffen. Properly prepared, hydraulic lime mixes should have relatively low shrinkage.

Natural ('Roman') cements

Natural cements can be described as a class of hydraulic materials between eminently hydraulic limes and modern artificial cements. They are produced by burning argillaceous limestones like septaria which contain an extremely high proportion of clay (30-55%) as well as some iron oxide. Unlike hydraulic limes, calcined natural cements cannot slake in lump form and must be ground before use. Natural cements will set very rapidly under water (in 15 minutes to one hour) and can attain quite high strengths. They will vary in colour from light yellow to dark brown depending on the content of iron oxide in the raw material.

Natural cements were developed at the end of the eighteenth century in the wave of experimentation with hydraulic materials that eventually led to the creation of artificial cements (like Portland cement). 'Roman Cement' was the name given to a natural cement developed by James Parker in 1796 from septaria of the Isle of Sheppey. However, the term came to be used in a generic way to describe similar natural cement products.

Although natural cements were once produced at a number of locations in the UK, there is no longer any domestic production and all such materials are now imported.

Pozzolanic additives

Certain materials, known as 'pozzolans' or 'pozzolanic additives', will react with non-hydraulic lime in the presence of water to produce a hydraulic set. The term derives from perhaps the best known of these materials, a volcanic ash called *pozzolana* found in the region of Pozzuoli (hence its name) near Naples, which has been used since Roman times to produce hydraulic mortars. Other natural pozzolans include trass from the Rhine region in Germany, pumice, and the tuff of the Greek island Santorini.

In addition to natural pozzolans, the Romans also used artificial pozzolanic materials such as crushed bricks and tiles to produce a hydraulic set in mortars. Like the natural pozzolans, all such materials contain reactive silica and alumina which, in the presence of water, react with lime.

Contemporary practice in Britain makes use of various materials as pozzolanic additives in lime mortars. These include crushed brick dust, HTI powder (prepared from refractory bricks used for high temperature insulation), and PFA (pulverised fuel ash) of low sulphate content.

The choice of a pozzolan will depend on the required hydraulicity as well as factors such as the colour (and other properties) they may impart to a mortar or render. Considerable care must be exercised when specifying such materials. It should be noted, for example, that not all brick dusts are pozzolanic. Recent research has shown that the most reactive brick dusts are obtained from low-fired bricks (fired at temperatures below 900°C) which are crushed to produce particles smaller than 75 microns. HTI powder has also been shown to vary in hydraulicity, possibly because of variations in firing temperature. It is therefore very important to test any proposed pozzolan for its hydraulicity before recommending its general use.

Recently, new 'pozzolanic' materials such as GGBS (Ground Granulated Burnt Slag) and a reactive metakaolin (produced from calcined china clay) have become available in the marketplace. However, these materials have not been extensively tested for their appropriateness in conservation work and further research is needed before they can be generally recommended.

Surface finishes

Limewash

Limewash is a traditional surface finish for lime plaster, limestone, daubs and earth walls. The most basic limewash is composed simply of slaked lime and water. However, materials such as tallow, casein or linseed oil are often added to create a more durable and water-resistant treatment (particularly for external use). Similarly, appropriate (lime-fast) pigments may be added for colour.

Limewashes may be prepared on site from the necessary raw materials or purchased premixed with various binders and pigments. When mixing on site, it is best to prepare a limewash from either quicklime or lime putty. Limewash prepared from ordinary hydrated lime (dry hydrate or bag lime) will be of inferior quality and limited durability.

Sources of further information on making and applying limewash are provided in the bibliography. Details of particular products can be obtained from the suppliers.

Distempers

The term *distemper* originally referred to water-soluble paints which dried by evaporation. These traditional or 'soft' distempers were mostly based on whiting (very finely pulverised chalk or chemically precipitated calcium carbonate) mixed with glue size in hot water. This basic mix could then be tinted with coloured pigments to create a range of colours.

Later, drying oils were added to create emulsions that dried by oxidation. These oil-bound or 'washable' distempers were the precursors of modern emulsion paints.

The directory (Chapter 2) lists a number of suppliers of both soft (glue-size) and oil-bound distempers, as well as other lime-based paints. Where the exact components of a product are not clear or additives are not specified, further information should be requested from the supplier. Sources of further information on the production and use of distempers are provided in the bibliography (Chapter 4).

LIME CHARACTERISATION

LIME CLASSIFICATION	ACTIVE CLAY MATERIALS	SETTING TIME IN WATER	SLAKING TIME	EXPANSION ON SLAKING	TYPICAL COLOURS
FAT (also described as PURE or HIGH CALCIUM)	<6% (typically <2%)	NO SET (PUTTY)	VERY FAST	CONSIDERABLE	WHITE
LEAN	<12% (typically <6%)	NO SET (PUTTY)	FAST	LARGE (eg, x2)	WHITE OFF-WHITE
MAGNESIAN (DOLOMITIC)	<30% (typically <10%)	NO SET (PUTTY)	VERY SLOW	VARIES, CAN BE CONSIDERABLE	WHITE OFF-WHITE
FEEBLY HYDRAULIC	<12%	>20 DAYS	SLOW	SLIGHT	OFF-WHITE, PALE GREY
MODERATELY HYDRAULIC	12%-18%	15-20 DAYS	SLOW	SLIGHT	PALE GREY, PALE BUFF
EMINENTLY HYDRAULIC	18%-25%	2-4 DAYS	VERY SLOW	SLIGHT	GREY, DARK GREY, BROWN
NATURAL CEMENTS	30%-55%	2-12 HOURS	NO SLAKING; CLINKER MUST BE GROUND	NONE	LIGHT TO VERY DARK BROWN

TABLE 1
Adapted from J. Ashurst, Mortars, *Plasters and Renders in Conservation*,
acknowledgement to L. J. Vicat (1837), A. D. Cowper (1927), M. Wingate and S. Holmes (1996).

Chapter 2

Alphabetical Directory of Producers and Suppliers

This section lists producers and suppliers of bagged dry hydrate limes, lime putties, quicklime, ready-mixed lime/sand mortars, limewashes and related products for use in lime mortars, renders and plasters.

The entries in this directory have been compiled on the basis of information from the producers and suppliers. The sample prices are exclusive of VAT and delivery unless otherwise stated, and are correct at the time of preparation (Summer 1996). The products, quantities and prices shown in the directory entries are included as guides to what each company has to offer, not complete product catalogues. When comparing products and prices, please bear in mind that not all suppliers quote on the basis of the same measurements of quantity (some suppliers favour kilograms, for example, while others quote according to packaging method). There may be discounts available on bulk orders, or surcharges on small quantities. Delivery charges will add to the cost of an order, and prices may also vary according to the availability of raw materials.

While every effort has been made to ensure that the information given in this directory is correct, mistakes may occur and circumstances may have changed since going to press. Readers are therefore advised that they deal with the suppliers and contractors listed here at their own risk. Samples should be requested and current prices confirmed with suppliers before any firm orders are placed.

The publishers would be most grateful if readers would make any errors or omissions known to them so that the information contained in this directory can be updated in future editions. Please use the form on page 59 to send in your comments and suggestions.

England

A

ARC Southern
Frome Sales Office
Garston Road
Frome
Somerset
BA11 1RS

Tel: **(01373) 453333**
Fax: **(01373) 452964**

ARC Southern are producers of burnt lime, ground limestone ($CaCO_3$) and agricultural limestone (ground, screened and magnesian). Lime/sand mortars are also available: contact (01622) 679461.

Arnold & Gould
Horsehair Factories
Bells Lane
Glemsford
Sudbury
Suffolk
CO10 7QA

Tel: **(01787) 280343**
Fax: **(01787) 280986**

Horsehair supplied in any amount required.

Product	Quantity	£.p
Horsehair	kg	5.85

Ashfield Traditional
Cricketers
Forward Green
Stowmarket
Suffolk
IP14 5HP

Tel/Fax:
(01449) 711273

A supplier of traditional limewash derived from Buxton quicklime which has been slaked and passed through a very fine sieve. Ashfield Traditional make limewashes in interior and exterior grades in a range of traditional colours and pastel shades. Colour charts are available. One 15 litre tub covers up to 60 square metres. Full application guidance is provided with the product. The company is happy to discuss any queries.

Product	Quantity	£.p
Limewash	15 litre	18.50
Coloured limewash	15 litre	27.75
Tallow limewash	15 litre	20.50
Coloured tallow limewash	15 litre	29.75
Pigments (various colours)	kg	from 7.50
Hair (goat/horse)	kg	from 7.50

(prices are inclusive of VAT)

Bleaklow Industries Ltd.
Hassop Avenue
Hassop
Derbyshire
DE45 1NS

Tel: **(01246) 582284**
Fax: **(01246) 583192**

Bleaklow Industries Ltd. supply a very fine ground, matured, flexible slaked lime putty and ready-to-use lime/sand mortars made to order and three standard mixes. A brochure is available, containing information on the different applications of slaked lime. Supplied direct from manufacturer at wholesale prices, the lime is 96% calcium oxide, slaked fresh.

Product	Quantity	£.p
Slaked lime putty	25 litre tub	8.75
	24 tubs (pallet)	210.00

Blue Circle Industries Plc
Head Office
Blue Circle Cement
Portland House
Church Road
Aldermaston
Berkshire
RG7 4HP

Tel: **(01189) 818000**
Fax: **(01189) 818399**

Blue Circle supplies large quantities of hydrated lime to builders merchants from regional offices at South Glamorgan, Stoke-on-Trent, Manchester, Suffolk, Kent, Belfast, Plymouth, Glasgow, Newcastle-upon-Tyne, Wiltshire and Nottinghamshire. The Blue Circle product is called 'Hydralime', a high calcium, non-hydraulic, hydrated lime which complies with the requirements of BS890 'Specification for Building Limes'.

Hydralime is for use with Ordinary Portland cement in mortars, plaster and renders. The maximum benefit is obtained when the product is added to water, stirred constantly to mix and then allowed to stand in water for 24 hours before use.

Hydralime is delivered throughout the UK in 25 kg-sized bags at £110-£115 per tonne, depending on haulage charges. Further information can be obtained from the technical representatives at the regional offices.

Building Conservation Services
Horbury Hall
Church Street
Horbury
Wakefield
WF4 6LT

Tel: **(01924) 277552**
Fax: **(01924) 277552**

Building Conservation Services supply a range of slaked lime products for use in traditional buildings. In addition to lime putty, they supply ready-mixed lime plaster and mortars, including a 1:4 lime/sand mix designed to be mixed with cement or another pozzolanic additive to achieve a quicker set. They also offer lime ash, a mixture of lime, ash and gypsum that was widely used in post-medieval buildings as a floor screed.

Product	Quantity	£.p
Lime putty	75 kg*	20.00
Traditional lime mortar	100 kg	24.50
Lime mortar (for gauging with cement/pozzolanic additive)	100 kg	24.50
Ready-mixed lime plaster	100 kg	26.60
Crushed brick	50 kg	12.00

Goat hair	kg	1.35
Laths (oak or chestnut)	per foot	0.35
Lime ash (3-pack repair mix; covers 1-1.5 sq. m)		90.00

* A refundable deposit of £5.00 is payable on 75 kg and 100 kg drums.

Bursledon Brickworks
(The Centre for the
Conservation of the Built
Environment)
Coal Park Lane
Swanwick
Southampton
SO31 7GW

Tel: **(01489) 584613**
Tel/Fax:
(01489) 576248

Contact: Kevin Stubbs

The Hampshire Buildings Preservation Trust runs the Centre for the Conservation of the Built Environment from a historic brickworks in Bursledon, with grant aid from Hampshire County Council, Redland Plc and others. The Centre stocks lime putties, mortars and washes, Jurakalk hydraulic lime, hair, stone dust, pigments and pointing irons. Timber products include air-dried oak and laths.

Surplus income from the sale of building materials and tools is covenanted to the Trust, to enable it to continue its educational and conservation work. Please ask for a complete list of products and prices.

Product	Quantity	£.p
Cheddar mortar grade lime putty	30 litre tub	12.50
Shillingstone lime putty (feebly hydraulic)	30 litre tub	13.50
Buxton superfine lime putty	30 litre tub	17.50
Jurakalk eminently hydraulic lime	40 kg sack	15.50
Ready-mixed lime mortars		
Standard coarse stuff	30 litre tub	9.25
Extra coarse stuff (for flint work)	30 litre tub	9.50
Coarse stuff with chalk (for cob render)	30 litre tub	10.00
Coarse stuff with hair	25 kg bag	6.50
Finishing stuff	25 kg bag	5.25
Special mixes (e.g. Devon red)	25 kg bag	5.50
Limewash	25 kg bag	8.50
Laths (3 feet, 3.5 feet and 4 feet lengths)		
Riven oak	per foot	0.30
Riven chestnut	per foot	0.25

Animal hair, stone dust, pigments and pozzolanic and other additives are also available.
Prices depend on type, colour and quantity.

**Buxton Lime
Industries Ltd.**

Tunstead Quarry
Wormhill
Near Buxton
Derbyshire

Tel (general enquiries):
(01298) 768444
Quicklime:
(01298) 768462
Technical marketing
co-ordinator:
(01298) 768481
Hydrated lime (bulk):
(01298) 768349
Hydrated lime (packed):
(01298) 768307

Fax: **(01298) 769334**

Buxton Lime Industries (BLI) Ltd. has been manufacturing lime-based products since the 1890s. BLI, formerly the Lime Products business of Imperial Chemical Industries, is a core part of Minorco Industrial Minerals and operates from two sites near Buxton in Derbyshire. It supplies hydrated lime and quicklime, in either bulk or bagged forms, to a wide variety of building and construction companies and to many manufacturers of proprietary putties, mortars and limewashes.

BLI's quicklime is a white to off-white solid of angular particle shape. The product is quite friable and usually has a dusty appearance. It is available in the following grades: Lump 40 (nominally -40 +20 mm), Granula 15 (nominally sizes of -20 +6 mm), Fine 6 (nominally -10 +0 mm) or in powder form. Lump quicklime is normally delivered in bulk tippers. Granular quicklime and fine quicklime can be carried by either tippers or air pressure delivery road tankers. All grades can be made available in 25 kg plastic sacks or 1 tonne flexible intermediate bulk containers on request.

BLI's 'Limbux' hydrated lime or slaked lime is manufactured at Tunstead works near Buxton, Derbyshire. 'Limbux' hydrated lime is a fine white, dry powder of pure and consistent quality consisting mainly of calcium hydroxide. The median particle size is approximately 8 microns. 'Limbux' is supplied in bulk via air pressure delivery road tankers or in paper sacks of approximately 25 kg each, delivered on pallets holding a nominal 1 tonne, shrink-wrapped if required. It is also supplied in woven flexible intermediate bulk containers, polythene lined, of nominal 750 kg or 1 tonne capacity.

A technical enquiries service is available. Prices vary according to product, package type and offtake and are available on request.

**Cathedral Works
Organisation
(Chichester) Ltd.**

Terminus Road
Chichester
West Sussex
PO19 2TX

Tel: **(01243) 784225**
Fax: **(01243) 813700**

Cathedral Works Organisation supplies an imported product called 'French Natural Hydraulic Lime XHN30', which compares closely with the once well-known British hydraulic limes such as the Blue Lias, Holywell or Rugby and is mixed in similar proportions for renders and mortars, such as 1:2.5, 1:3 and 1:4. XHN30 will develop an initial set in a few hours, but will harden progressively over a long period of time. This slow hardening process prevents many of the problems associated with quick-setting cements, such as shrinkage, cracking and poor bonding. The pale, off-white colour of XHN30 is an attractive alternative to the dead whiteness of non-hydraulic lime and the greyness of Ordinary Portland cement.

Product	Quantity	£.p
Natural Hydraulic Lime XHN30	40 kg bag	8.98
	pallet (1 tonne load)	224.00
Slaked lime putty	25 litre tub	14.75
Bath stone dust (fine)	25 kg bag	7.50
Bath stone dust (coarse)	25 kg bag	7.50
Portland stone dust (fine)	25 kg bag	7.50
Portland stone dust (coarse)	25 kg bag	7.50
HTI powder (kiln dust)	25 kg bag (approx)	24.70
Template material (orange plastic)	83m x 1.2m roll	196.00

H. J. Chard & Sons
Albert Road
Bristol
Avon
BS2 0XS

Tel. (Builders
Merchants):
(0117) 9777681
Tel. (Mechanical
Engineers):
(0117) 9717341

H. J. Chard & Sons manufacture and sell direct to trade and retail outlets lime putty made from Buxton non-hydraulic white quicklime. The lime putty serves as the base for the production of a range of lime/sand mortars which can be made to order. Pigments available include yellow, brown umber, red, black, marigold, terracotta, light brown, red brown and lilac.

Product	Quantity	£.p
Lime putty	40 kg tub	9.00
	tonne (loose)	95.00
Lump lime	40 kg bag	5.80
Hydrated lime	25 kg bag	2.95
Tallow (for use with lump lime:	1 kg bag	1.60
1kg per 50 kg lime)	20 kg box	23.26
Raw linseed oil (for use with lime putty:	300 ml	1.20
300ml per 40 kg tub)	2 litre	6.10
HTI Powder	25 kg bag	18.50
Plasterers' hair	kg	2.30
(5 kg hair per 1 ton lime putty)	5 kg bag	11.50
Laths	3 foot bundle	37.50
	4 foot bundle	50.00
	foot	0.25
Pigments	1 kg bag	from 1.50
	8 kg bag	from 10.00
	25 kg bag	from 16.40

Cornish Lime Company
Brims Park
Old Callywith Road
Bodmin
Cornwall
PL31 2DZ

Tel: **(01208) 79779**
Fax: **(01208) 73744**

Contact: P. Brown

Founded in 1994, the Cornish Lime Company manufactures lime putty, limewash and ready-mixed mortars and plasters. Lime putty is left a minimum of three months before use or sale. Pozzolans are available ex stock, along with hair, tallow, casein, lime fast pigments, and large or small quantities of grouting medium. The company maintains an extensive sand library of West Country aggregates and offers a basic mortar analysis service, which is free of charge on orders over £100.00. All prices are subject to quantity discount.

Product	Quantity	£.p
Lime putty	30 litre (40 kg)	9.50
Limewash	30 litre	15.00
Limewash (coloured)	30 litre	19.50
Limewash (oilbound)	30 litre	19.00
Lime mortar	50 kg bag	6.00
(3:1 common mix 'coarse stuff')	1 tonne	110.00
Coloured (natural sands) **mortars**	50 kg bag	6.50

Cy-Pres
14 Bells Close
Brigstock
Kettering
Northamptonshire
NN14 3JG

Tel: **(01536) 373431**

Cy-Pres are specialist suppliers and contractors for the repair and maintenance of historic buildings. They supply and apply a great variety of traditional building materials and decorative finishes, including pre-mixed lime putty, limewashes, and lime/sand mortars to specification for individual requirements. Cy-Pres mortars are manufactured using slaked, non-hydraulic lime which has been allowed to mature for at least six weeks as lime putty. Their soft distemper is made in the traditional way, using 'best town whiting', glue-size binder and specially selected natural earth pigments for colouring.

An analysis and mortar matching service is free on orders over £25.00. Further technical assistance is available on request. A contracting service is also available to supply and apply Cy-Pres products.

Product	Quantity	£.p
Standard mortar	50 kg keg	10.00
Pozzolanic mortar	50 kg keg	12.00
Medium-coarse render	50 kg keg	10.00
Fine finish (unhaired)	50 kg keg	12.00
Fine finish (with hair)	50 kg keg	12.00
Internal and external limewash (white)	10 litre	10.00

Internal and external limewash (pale colours)	10 litre	12.00
Coloured brickwash	10 litre	12.00
Traditional soft distemper (white)	5 litre	14.00
Traditional soft distemper (coloured)	5 litre	20.00

Dolmen
Vernacular Building
Materials and
Conservation
Consultants
Learoyd Road
Mountfield Industrial
Estate
New Romney
Kent
TN28 8XU

Tel: **(01797) 367543**
Fax: **(01797) 367136**

Dolmen supply tubs of mature lime putty, ready-mixed lime mortars, limewash and pigments, linseed oil, cleft and sawn laths, specialist tools and sundries. The company also offers a mortar analysis service.

Prices are available on application. Delivery is available throughout the South-east.

Farrow & Ball Ltd.
Manufacturers of
Specialist and
Traditional Paint
Uddens Trading Estate
Wimborne
Dorset
BH12 7NL

Tel: **(01202) 876141**
Fax: **(01202) 873793**

Farrow & Ball manufacture a full range of traditional paints including limewash, based on a formula of slaked lime ready for dilution for an application to porous fabric. May be used on interior and exterior plastered and rendered walls. Brochure and technical data sheets available free of charge.

Factory strength water stainers for limewash are available in White, Yellow Ochre, Raw Umber, Burnt Umber, Burnt Sienna, Black, Lime Yellow, Blue and Red. Orders are delivered in the UK within 3-5 working days. Export delivery and express services are available by arrangement.

Product	Quantity	£.p
Limewash (white only)	5 litre	13.69

Price includes delivery to mainland UK.

W. Fein & Sons Ltd.
Park View Mills
Raymond Street
Bradford
BD5 8DT

Tel: **(01274) 730760**
Fax: **(01274) 722904**

Product	Quantity	£.p
Goat hair	kg	1.00

Minimum order: 50 kg.

A. E. Griffin & Son
Bere Regis
Wareham
Dorset
BH20 7LA

Tel: **(01929) 471253**
Fax: **(01929) 472208**

A. E. Griffin & Son, builders and specialists in the care of historic buildings, produce lime putty using quicklime from Cheddar, Somerset. Related products and additives, such as tallow, oils, pigments, brickdust and trass, are also available.

Hendry & Sons Ltd.
Station Road
Foulsham
Dereham
Norfolk
NR20 5RG

Tel: **(01362) 683249**

Builders and contractors, suppliers of slaked lime putty from Buxton quicklime, lime-sand mortars, limewash and weavers' hair as well as products used for the storage and application of lime materials.

Product	Quantity	£.p
Slaked lime putty	25 litre drum	12.50
Limewash (ready-to-use)	11 gallon bin	37.00
Pigment powders		
Raw sienna	kg	9.50
Umber	kg	4.50
Yellow ochre	kg	8.00
Burnt sienna	kg	9.00
Red ochre	kg	9.00
Vegetable black	kg	8.50
Hair (weavers' clippings)	lb	3.00
Fine lime mortar	60 litre	40.00
Coarse mortar without hair	60 litre	24.00
Coarse mortar with hair	60 litre	36.00
Chestnut laths	sawn bundle	20.00

(20 No. 5 feet 6 inches – i.e. 1.68m)

1 inch sheradised nails (for laths)	kg	2.50
Building clay (bagged)	cwt	4.50
Bristle brushes for scrubbing walls	each	4.00
Limewash brushes (100mm by 50mm)	each	3.50

Hirst Conservation Materials Ltd.
Laughton
Sleaford
Lincolnshire
NG34 0HE

Tel: **(01529) 497517**
Fax: **(01529) 497518**

Hirst Conservation Materials Ltd. is a producer and supplier of a wide range of lime products and related services. Products include lime putty, mixed mortars, plasters, renders, daubs and grouts for building repair. The company also makes historical mortars, plasters, coatings and paints. Traditional coatings and paints made with lead, zinc, soft distemper and milk paint (casein/oil-bound distemper) are also supplied. Technical advice on the use of products is available, as well as a materials analysis and research service. Full details of products and services are given in free literature.

The company is a subsidiary of the Hirst Conservation contracting company, which carries out a wide range of conservation projects.

Product	Quantity	£.p
Limewater	*	9.88
Limewash	*	11.86
Tinted limewash	*	p.o.a.
Coloured limewash	*	p.o.a.
Lime putty	*	11.20
Fine stuff	*	16.37
Coarse stuff	*	14.37
Coarse stuff with hair	*	19.61
Daub	*	29.16
Lime putty in bulk	500 litre box	170.00
Coarse mortar in bulk	500 litre box	200.00

* Pallet rate per bucket. A premium is charged for smaller quantities. European and international deliveries can be arranged.

Hydraulic Lias
Limes Ltd.
Melmoth House
Abbey Close
Sherborne
Dorset
DT9 3LH

Tel: **(01935) 817220**
Fax: **(01935) 817222**

Lime Plant:
Tel: **(01458) 223179**

Blue Lias hydraulic lime was traditionally the pre-eminent hydraulic lime of England. In May 1994, after half a century during which it had not been produced in this country, blue Lias lime was reintroduced by Somerset Stonework Ltd. A new company, Hydraulic Lias Limes Ltd., started trading in October 1994.

The lime sets quickly – the same day in the open and in three days underwater. It is pale cream in colour and is manufactured as a fine hydrated powder which is used in a similar way to Ordinary Portland cement. Tests to date show a compressive strength of 2.5 newtons/mm^2 on 1:3 mortar after 6 months. The material has been successfully used on conservation projects and has also been specified for new work.

Fat lime putty production began in 1996. The directors are pursuing a policy of continuous product development. They are confident the limes manufactured by the company are the finest traditional building limes available anywhere in Europe. General information, fact sheets and brochures can be obtained from the office address.

I.J.P. Building
Conservation
Hollow Tree Cottage
Binfield Heath
Nr Henley-on-Thames
Oxfordshire
RG9 4LR

Tel: **(01734) 462697**
Fax: **(01734) 463744**

Suppliers of carboniferous non-hydraulic lime slaked in putties or mixed in mortars, plasters and limewashes. Range includes extra coarse mix (suitable for laying flints, rough stone and brick work or as a coarse render coat); coarse stuff and fine stuff (suitable for laying bricks, stones, pointing, plastering or rendering); a daub mix, without straw (suitable for infills for timber framed buildings, for use in the repair of existing panels or making new panels). Extra fine, lime-rich or special mixes are available on request. Large quantities can be mixed on site. Pigments suitable for limewashes, mortars and plasters can be supplied: prices vary, depending on colour and quantity.

Product	Quantity	£.p
Extra coarse mix	25 litre drum	14.00
Coarse stuff	25 litre drum	11.00
Fine stuff	25 litre drum	20.00
Lime putty (slaked)	25 litre tub	11.00
Limewash	25 litre tub	20.00
Limewash	5 litre tub	5.00
Daub mixes	25 litre tub	18.00

Goat, horse and cow hair (other types available)

Uncut horse tail hair	kg	6.00
Cut horse mane	kg	9.00
Cut goat hair	kg	9.00
Uncut goat hair	kg	8.00
Uncut cow tail hair	kg	8.00
Beeswax	200g block	3.60
	kg	13.00
Raw linseed oil	500 ml	3.60
	litre	4.90
Boiled linseed oil	500 ml	3.60
	litre	5.30

Liz Induni
11 Park Road
Swanage
Dorset
BH19 2AA

Tel: **(01929) 423776**

Product	Quantity	£.p
Limewash (white)	15 litre tub	15.00
Limewash (coloured)	15 litre tub	20.00
Pigments		p.o.a.

J. Layzell & Sons
Stoneleigh
Horton
Ilminster
Somerset
TA19 9QT

Tel: **(01460) 52855**
Fax: **(01460) 52152**

Founded in 1895, J. Layzell & Sons specialise in the repair and conservation of historic buildings. They supply all lime products, pozzolans, hair, natural earth pigments and grouting medium.

Product	Quantity	£.p
Lime putty	30 litre (40 kg)	11.00
Limewash (white)	30 litre	16.00
Limewash (coloured)	30 litre	22.00
Lime mortar	30 litre (40 kg)	9.00
	1 tonne	100.00
Brick dust	50 kg	20.00
Lias hydraulic lime	25 kg	13.00
French hydraulic lime	50 kg	19.00

All prices subject to quantity discounts, ex works.

The Lime Centre
Long Barn
Morestead
Winchester
Hampshire
SO21 1LZ

Tel: **(01962) 713636**
Fax: **(01962) 715350**

Contact: R. H. Bennett

The Lime Centre offers practical training, material supplies, mortar analysis service and consultancy to professionals, building owners and contractors. Consultancy includes evaluation of buildings, examination of existing mortars, plasters and renders, and recommendations for the preparation of matching materials.

Product	Quantity	£.p
Lime putty*		
Extra mature (over 3 yrs old)	17 litre tub	p.o.a.
Standard mature	17 litre tub	p.o.a.
Lime mortar* (coarse and fine)	20 litre tub	p.o.a.
Limewash (plain or with various binders)	5 litre tub	p.o.a.
	10 litre tub	p.o.a.
Hydraulic and Eminently Hydraulic Lime (Jurakalk and St. Astier)		p.o.a.

* Bulk supplies available.
10 days' notice is required on pigmented limewash orders.
Riven laths, animal hair, specialist tools etc. also available. Contact Bob Bennett for details.

**Limebase
Products Ltd.**
Walronds Park
Isle Brewers
Taunton
Somerset
TA3 6QP

Tel/Fax:
(01460) 281921

This small and expanding company was set up in 1994 to supply locally-derived and produced, lime-based materials to masons, plasterers, builders, conservators and home owners in Somerset and the South West. In 1995, Nick Durnan joined the company as a consultant. His 20 years of experience in the conservation of historic stonework enables the company to offer advice concerning the repair of historic stonework and plasterwork, as well as a mortar analysis and matching service.

Besides the products listed below, Limebase sell Ham stone, Bath Stone and Lias mortars, a complete range of lime additives, a variety of stone dusts and sands, tools and brushes.

Product	Quantity	£.p
Lime putty	30 litre tub	10.35
Quick (lump) **lime**	10 kg bag	2.95
Mature lime putty (over one year old)	10 litre tub	8.95
Limewash (white)	10 litre tub	10.50
Limewash (standard colours)	10 litre	14.10
Ready-mixed mortar	tonne	90.00
	25 kg bag	3.95

Roughcast plaster	25 kg bag	3.95
Hair plaster	25 kg bag	4.50
Finish plaster	25 kg bag	5.45

£2.00 refund on each container returned in good, clean condition.

Lawrence Long Ltd.
27 Vaughton Street
South
Birmingham
B12 0YN

Tel: **(0121) 6223114**
Fax: **(0121) 6281994**

Bass, fibre & horse hair dressers established in 1921.

Product	Quantity	£.p
Plasterers' hair	kg	6.65

Mascot Traditional Materials
Owl's House
Frieston Road
Caythorpe
Grantham
Lincolnshire
NG32 3BX

Tel: **(01400) 272724**
Fax: **(01400) 273628**

Contact:
Isabel Welby-Everard

From 1992 to March 1996, Isabel Welby-Everard was involved in a company supplying lime products to companies, architects and private individuals. Having gained a great deal of knowledge from various experts in this field, she decided to set up her own business.

Mascot Traditional Materials aim to give a high standard of service to clients in selecting the best available material in terms of suitability, quality and price. Lime is a simple product, but the importance of choosing the correct lime and correct application cannot be overstressed.

Prices vary, but Mascot Traditional Materials can obtain for their customers the best available price based on quality and quantity.

J. Negus
11A St. Johns Road
Hampton Wick
Kingston
Surrey
KT1

Tel/Fax:
(0181) 9770816

Jem Negus stocks Bleaklow's matured slaked lime putty and ready-mixed coarse, medium and fine mortars, and supplies them to London and the South-east.

Product	Quantity	£.p
Lime putty	25 litre tub	11.75
Coarse stuff	40 kg	9.40
Medium stuff	40 kg	9.40
Fine stuff	40 kg	9.40

Optiroc Ltd.
Adamson House
Pomona Strand
Throstle Nest Lane
Manchester
M16 0BA

Tel: **(0161) 8760699**
Fax: **(0161) 8720736**

Optiroc Ltd. (formerly Serpo UK Ltd.) is a subsidiary of Scancem ab. The Scancem company supplies building materials and industrial minerals to all parts of the world. The company has been selling products for over 70 years and continues to sell a wide range of lime-based products, including Gotland lime paint, hydraulic lime mortar (fine), roughcast hydraulic lime rendering, hydraulic lime grout, roughcast lime rendering and lime paint for lime-finished facades.

Optiroc products are available through approved contractors who are located throughout the UK and Scotland. The Manchester office can offer guideline prices and prepare work specifications.

Papers and Paints Ltd.
4 Park Walk
London
SW10 0AD

Tel: **(0171) 3528626**
Fax: **(0171) 3521017**

Papers and Paints is a long-established family company, selling a complete range of traditional colours and modern paints and finishes. Superfine lime putty and a range of pigments are sold, and advice given to customers who wish to mix limewashes for decorating or restoration projects.

Product	Quantity	£.p
Superfine lime putty	25 litre tub	21.00
Earth pigments	500 grams	from 4.10

Potmolen Lime
Traditional Lime Mortars
27 & 41 Woodcock
Industrial Estate
Warminster
Wiltshire
BA12 9DX

Tel: **(01985) 213960**
Fax: **(01985) 213931**

Potmolen Lime offer mortars, renders, and plasters (with or without hair) and shelter coats made with extra-fine mature lime putty. All lime putty is guaranteed at least 12 weeks old. Special mixes can be supplied to order. Prices and mixes on application.

Potmolen Paint
Traditional and
Natural Paints
27 Woodcock Industrial
Estate
Warminster
Wiltshire
BA12 9DX

Tel: **(01985) 213960**
Fax: **(01985) 213931**

Potmolen are established suppliers of a wide variety of finish coatings and paints for traditional and contemporary buildings, including distemper, linseed oil paint and lead paint, pigment washes and non-toxic, water-thinnable finishes for timber. Limewash is available in 10 litre and 25 kg sizes in a wide range of light, traditional colours. Colour charts are available on request. Powder pigments, raw oil and tallow are also available.

A new, water-thinnable, non-toxic lime wall paint is now available, called 'Chapel Coat'. Based on pure lime putty, it is suitable for exterior and interior use and serves as a spatchel filler on many porous surfaces. It has a high degree of vapour permeability and may be used as a ready-mixed skim coat in lime plasterwork. Spreading rate: approximately 5 to 10 square metres per litre.

Potmolen Paint are the UK agent for White Rhino Lime (Clogrennane Lime Ltd.). All lime putty is guaranteed at least 12 weeks old.

Product	Quantity	£.p
Extra fine mature lime putty (white)	10 litre	11.70
Extra fine mature lime putty (with oil)	10 litre	24.07
Extra fine mature lime putty (coloured)	10 litre	27.27
Chapel coat (white only)	10 litre	40.11

Rates for pallets and 25 kg tubs are available on request.

**The Real Paint &
Varnish Company**
3 Meal Bank Mill
Kendal
Cumbria
LA8 9DW

Tel/Fax:
(01539) 721992

Contact: Peter Hood

The Real Paint & Varnish Company specialise in the manufacture of genuine historic painting and decorating materials, as much for the serious restorer as for today's artists and craftsmen. The wide range includes lime-based coatings and appropriate preparation materials. Ingredients, including natural earths for colouring, are processed in house to guarantee quality, integrity and authenticity. All products are supported by technical information and practical guidance, including direction on regulations, application and maintenance. Advice on conservation, research, analysis, interpretation and historic colours is available. The company is committed to a policy of environmental awareness. Courses run by Peter Hood on the history of decoration and painting include the use of lime in plasters, paints and coatings.

Product	Quantity	£.p
Limewash (white)	5 litre	7.50
Lime distemper	5 litre	14.00
Badigeon (stone white)	5 litre	6.90
Lime paint (white)	5 litre	22.50

Historic and vernacular colours are available to order.

Elaine Rigby and Charles Blackett-Ord
Intake Side
Brough
Kirkby Stephen
Cumbria
CA17 4EA

Tel/Fax:
(017683) 52572

Contact: Elaine Rigby or Charles Blackett-Ord

Elaine Rigby and Charles Blackett-Ord supply mature slaked lime putty from Kirkby Stephen (minimum 2 years old) and Shap lump lime, goat hair and pigments throughout the North of England. Lime putty is supplied in 30 kg bags.

Training courses are regularly held at Brough. On-site training can also be provided in the North of England (tailor-made, one-day courses are a speciality) or the role of working advisor can be undertaken on specific projects. Advice on suppliers of bulk materials, aggregates and putty is also available.

As architects and engineers, Elaine Rigby and Charles Blackett-Ord have broad experience of the repair and conservation of historic buildings and particularly the vernacular architecture of the North through an extensive list of completed projects and wide-ranging consultancy to other building professionals and national organisations.

RMC Industrial Minerals Ltd.
Hindlow
Buxton
Derbyshire
SK17 0EL

and

Hartley Quarry
Kirkby Stephen
Cumbria
CA17 4JJ

Tel:
(01298) 71155
Sales Office:
(01298) 25424
Fax:
(01298) 75792

At Hindlow Quarry, Buxton, Derbyshire, RMC Industrial Minerals Ltd. manufacture high quality lime products.

Quicklime (calcium oxide) is produced by the calcination of extremely high purity Derbyshire limestone using natural gas in one of the most modern processing plants in the world. Quicklime is crushed and graded into 7 sizes, from 175 mm to 1 mm and is also available ground into a fine powder.

Hydrated lime (calcium hydroxide) is produced at Hindlow and also at Hartley Quarry, Kirkby Stephen, Cumbria. The process involves mixing quicklime with water under highly controlled conditions to form a dry white powder.

Quicklime is delivered in tippers for lump and crushed lime and in air pressure discharge tankers for granular grades and powder.

Hydrated lime can be delivered palletised in 25 kg bags or IBC's and shrink-wrapped if required. Bulk delivery can be made by air pressure discharge tankers.

Rose of Jericho
at St. Blaise Ltd.
Westhill Barn
Evershot
Dorchester
Dorset
DT2 0LD

Tel: **(01935) 83676**
or **83662**
Fax: **(01935) 83017**
or **83676**

Contact: Pete Ellis

This maker of traditional mortars and paints supplies a wide range of products based on limes derived from non-hydraulic and hydraulic, British and European sources. A complete range of pozzolanic additives is also available.

Rose of Jericho supply a large standard range of lime putties (30 days mature minimum), mortars, plasters and renders suitable for all traditional building construction types, with full allowance for regional variations. Standard mixes, based on Cheddar lime, are supplied from stock; special and matching mortars within seven days. Special mortars include stone repair mixes, cobs, daubs, roughcasts and Roman cement. Lime mortars and plasters are supplied in 30 litre tubs, 25 kg or 1 tonne bags.

Four kinds of limewash and three distempers are supplied in a standard range of 100 traditional colours. Special colours can be mixed to order. A full mortar and paint analysis service, consultancy and advice are also available. Comprehensive information and instruction sheets for the use of each product are available on request.

Materials are exported to Europe, Africa, N. America and the Far East.

Products	Quantity	£.p
Lime putty*	30 litre (38 kg)	p.o.a.
Fat lime mortar grade (Cheddar)	tonne	230.00
Fat lime superfine (Buxton)	tonne	380.00
Lean lime (Shillingstone)	tonne	275.00
Lime Mortars and Plasters[†]		
1:3 (for bedding and pointing)	tonne	112.00
1:1.5 (for ashlar, fine bedding & pointing)	tonne	150.00
1:2 (for render and roughcast)	tonne	130.00
1:2.5 haired plaster	tonne	160.00
1:1 fine finish plaster	tonne	220.00
Limewashes		
Pure (white)	15 litre tub	17.50
Pure (coloured)	15 litre tub	22.50
Casein bound (white)	15 litre tub	27.50
Casein bound (coloured)	15 litre tub	32.50
with tallow/linseed oil (white)	15 litre tub	22.50
with tallow/linseed oil (coloured)	15 litre tub	27.50

* 30 days mature minimum. 100 day mature also available.
† Lean lime (Shillingstone) mortars and 100 days mature also available.
Trade and quantity discounts available. Carriage quoted individually.

**Severn Valley
Stone Co.**
63 Church Street
Tewkesbury
Gloucestershire
GL20 5RZ

Tel/Fax:
(01684) 297102
Yard: **(01684) 297060**
Mobile: **(0831) 888077**

Contact: Gary Coates

The Severn Valley Stone Co. offer 12-month-old, hand-slaked lime putty, in any quantity. The company also sell grey Forest of Dean stone for tiling roofs, dry walling and for carving. Prices vary according to availability. A countrywide delivery service is offered.

Product	Quantity	£.p
Lime putty	ton	200.00
Lime putty (fine meshed sieved)	ton	250.00
Ready-mixed mortar (to match existing)	ton	135.00
Earth mortar (to match existing)	ton	150.00
Limewash (all natural pigments available)	10 litre	10.00
Wattle panels	square metre	35.00
Daub (ready-to-use)	35 kg	35.00
Horse hair		p.o.a.
Goat hair		p.o.a.
Pig's blood	litre	5.00

J. & J. Sharpe
6 Clinton Gardens
Merton
Okehampton
Devon
EX20 3DP

Tel/Fax:
(01805) 603587

J. & J. Sharpe specialise in building repair and conservation, and supply lime products for use in the conservation of traditional stone and cob structures. The company manufacture and supply lime putty, mortar (approximately 300 tonnes in 1995). The standard mortar mix is 1 part lime: 3 parts pit sand; other mixes can be supplied on request and a mortar analysis service is available. One tub of plaster covers approximately 2 square metres at 10mm thick.

Product	Quantity	£.p
Lime putty	25 kg tub	6.00
	30 kg tub	7.00
Lime mortar/plaster (unhaired)	35 kg tub	6.00
Lime mortar/plaster (haired)	35 kg tub	7.00
Limewash (white)*	10 litre tub	5.00
Quicklime (15mm granular Buxton)	25 kg plastic bag	4.50

* Other colours are supplied to order.
Bulk 3 tonne loads can be delivered in skips. Discounts are available on large orders.

**Shillingstone Lime &
Stone Co. Ltd.**
Blandford Forum
Dorset
DT11 0TF

Tel: **(01258) 860338**

and

Buckland Newton
Dorchester
Dorset
DT2 7DN

Tel: **(01300) 345200**

Contact:
Rupert McCarthy or
Paul Simmons

The limeworks at Shillingstone are the only surviving example of a complete small-scale limeworks operating in the UK lime industry. The mixed feed, vertical shaft, draw arch, brick-built kilns have been continuously fired since 1924 and are the only kilns of this type known to be in regular operation in the UK. The Shillingstone Lime & Stone Co. Ltd. produce quicklime and hydrated lime. The hydrated lime is feebly hydraulic and is one of the only 'grey' hydrated limes in the UK, resembling the grey lime which was once produced at Totternhoe.

Product	Quantity	£.p
Quicklime, crushed or lump	50 kg sack	p.o.a.
Grey hydrated lime	ton	89.00

Singleton Birch Ltd.
Melton Ross Quarries
Barnetby
South Humberside
DN38 6AE

Tel: **(01652) 688386**
Fax: **(01652) 680485**

William Singleton Birch established the company in 1815 and developed the quarry and works into an important mineral industry in the nineteenth century. In 1856, when the Manchester, Sheffield and Lincolnshire railway was extended to Grimsby, the company acquired a small whiting works at Chalk Hill, Melton Ross. In the late 1950s lime kilns were added to the operation to develop the technique of burning lime and in 1964 the company's first slaking plant was commissioned to produce a high calcium hydrated lime powder in bulk or bags.

Melton Ross Quarries are located on a vast mineral deposit of high purity cretaceous chalk. The chalk is burnt and converted to burnt lime and discharged in cold lump form. Further crushing, screening and grading results in a variety of lime products from 40 mm lump to micron sized powders. Hydrated lime is also produced at the quarry site in a fine dry white powder form by slaking.

Product and technical data sheets and further information are available through the Technical Sales staff. Both the burnt and the hydrated lime are available in bulk tippers, air discharge tankers, IBC bags and 25 kg two-ply paper sacks. Prices depend on the grade of the product, packaging and delivery point and are quoted on request.

Speedlime
East Butts
Dunsford
Exeter
Devon
EX6 7DF

Tel: **(01647) 252161**

Speedlime supplies lime putty made from Buxton lime.

Product	Quantity	£.p
Lime putty	25 kg tub	6.25

Discounts available on orders over 20 tubs.

Tamar Trading Co. Ltd.
Builders Merchants
15 Bodmin Street
Holsworthy
Devon
EX22 6BB

Tel: **(01409) 253556**
Fax: **(01409) 254496**

Product	Quantity	£.p
Dry hydrated lime	25 kg bag	4.10
Lime putty	25 kg bag	9.50
1:6 lime/sand mortar	25 kg bag	2.00
Limewashes	25 kg bag	9.50
Tallow		p.o.a.
Hair		p.o.a.

Tec Build
Supplies Ltd.
PO Box 34
Tavistock
Devon
PL19 0XN

Tel: **(01822) 870405**
Fax: **(01822) 870605**

Managing Director:
Phil Northey

Tec Build is the only UK distributor for Rapide Natural Cement. The term 'Natural Cement' is used because Rapide is made simply from a particular type of clayey (argillaceous) limestone, found only in one seam in the Alps, which is fired and ground to produce a cement. Nothing is added, nothing is taken away.

Rapide, on its own, sets very quickly (in 90 seconds), and builds strength more slowly than conventional cements. It mixes very well with all types of lime and is used as an accelerator for lime renders and putties without affecting the qualities of the render in any other way.

Mix designs are available that enable the user to produce effective, waterproof, elastic renders that retain all the advantages of conventional lime but set far more quickly, thus allowing quicker working and their use in cold and wet weather. For further information and prices, please contact Phil Northey at Tec Build.

Telling Lime Products Ltd.
Primrose Avenue
Fordhouses
Wolverhampton
WV10 8AW

Tel: **(01902) 789777**
Fax: **(01902) 398777**

Contact: J.M. Parmley
(Marketing Manager)

Telling Lime Products carry a range of natural hydraulic lime available as bagged hydrate suitable for blending with customers' own aggregates to produce textures and colours required locally. In addition, more than 100 ready-mixed mortars, renders, grouts and plaster products are available, together with special damp course products. Renders and plasters are supplied in a range of natural colours and there is a wide range of coloured limewashes. Imitation polished marble finishes are also available. Free advice, site visits and specifications gladly given.

Product	Quantity	£.p
FEN X hydraulic lime hydrate	25 kg bag	p.o.a.
BIO E hydraulic lime hydrate	25 kg bag	p.o.a.
Unilit 20 lightweight insulating render	13 kg bag	p.o.a.
Unilit 35 premixed render/plaster	40 kg bag	p.o.a.
Unilit 30 premixed damp treatment	40 kg bag	p.o.a.
Unilit 45 premixed plaster/render finish	40 kg bag	p.o.a.
Unilit 40 premixed render finish	40 kg bag	p.o.a.
Unilit 300 coloured textured render finish	40 kg bag	p.o.a.
Unilit 400 coloured smooth render finish	40 kg bag	p.o.a.
Unilit 500 coloured polished finish	35 kg bag	p.o.a.
Cori limewash (range of colours)		p.o.a.
Unilit hydraulic lime paint (range of colours)		p.o.a.

Textured European Finishes Ltd.
1 Dunedin Road
Ilford
Essex
IG1 4LW

Tel: **(0181) 5531091**
Fax: **(0181) 4787870**

Contact: Cyril Wolffe
(Director)

Suppliers of a range of wall finish products, including the mineral coatings Vixalit, Visolcalce and Restaura Finish 05, which are imported from Italy.

Vixalit is described in the company's technical data sheet as an ecological, lime-based paint 'suitable for all interior and exterior mineral based substrates, such as rendered mortars, concretes and lime-based mortars. Especially indicated when one wants to attain a decorative surface with antique effects.' Vixalit is composed of well aged lime putty (from hydrated lime), natural pigments and additives.

Visolcalce is a trowel-applied coloured mineral wall coating in paste form, based on seasoned lime putty, selected marble powders, natural iron oxides, other inorganic, lime-resisting pigments and additives. Vixalit and Visolcalce are available in white and a range of pre-mixed colours.

Restaura Finish 05 is a lime-based thin rendering mortar supplied in powder form, composed of natural white hydraulic lime and selected extenders, recommended for levelling uneven surfaces and as a base for Vixalit and other mineral finishes.

Product	Quantity	£.p
Vixalit	25 kg drum	50.00
	5 kg drum	12.00
Visolcalce	25 kg drum	37.00
Restaura Finish 05	25 kg bag	22.00

Tilcon South Ltd.
Tunstead Quarry
Wormhill
Buxton
Derbyshire
SK17 8TG

Tel: **(01298) 768444**

Non-hydraulic lime/sand ready-mixed mortars are available from Tilcon at a number of depots throughout the UK, along with a cement-gauged lime/sand wet ready-mixed mortar which incorporates a 36-hour retarder. Tilcon also supply a lime aggregate plaster known as 'Limelite' plaster, which is supplied direct from Tilcon's Limelite Depot, at the address below.

Area Offices:

Tilcon North Ltd.
PO Box 5
Fell Bank
Birtley
Chester-le-Street
Co. Durham
DH3 2ST

Tel: **(0191) 4103180**

Tilcon Scotland
250 Alexandra
Parade
Glasgow
G31 3AX

Tel: **(0141) 5541818**

Limelite Depot
Doveholes Quarry
Dale Road
Doves Holes
Buxton
Derbyshire
SK17 8BQ

Tel: **(01298) 812386**

The Traditional Lime Co.
Church Farm
Leckhampton
Cheltenham
Gloucestershire
GL51 5XX

Tel: **(01242) 525444**
Fax: **(01242) 237727**

Contact:
Malcolm Wakeman

The Traditional Lime Co. supplies a range of high quality traditional lime products for the conservation and preservation of old buildings. Lime putties, slaked from highly reactive quicklime, are available in maturities from 3 months to 15 years. Lime mortars, renders, harlings, plasters, limewashes and natural pigments are available from stock.

Materials to match vernacular specifications are also prepared and a comprehensive technical service is provided which includes analysis of materials and on-site consultation.

Materials are packaged in 25 litre tubs and half, three-quarter or one tonne bags. Prices on application. Volume discounts are available.

Twyford Lime Products
Twyford Place
Tiverton
Devon
EX16 6AS

Tel/Fax:
(01884) 255407

Contact: Adrian Hunt

and

65 Old Town
Swindon
Wiltshire
SN3 1RT

Tel: **(01793) 521684**
Mobile: **(0802) 446433**

Contact: Adrian Daglish

Twyford Lime Products manufacture lime putty, limewashes and ready-mixed lime mortars and plasters – including lime skim for finish coats – for the repair of traditional cob and stone buildings. The lime putty is made from quicklime from Cheddar in Somerset and the company's own natural supply of untreated water. The standard lime mortar mix consists of 1 part lime putty to 3 parts sharp yellow sand from the South Somerset/East Devon area, but other mixes can be made up to match existing mortars (mortar analysis service available).

Limewashes are sold in plastic tubs of various sizes; all other products are packaged in 35 kg bags. For prices and further information, please contact Adrian Hunt or Adrian Daglish.

Weald & Downland
Open Air Museum
Singleton
Chichester
Sussex
PO18 0EU

Tel: **(01243) 811363**
Fax: **(01243) 811475**

Contact:
Christopher Zeuner

Suppliers of specialist materials for construction projects, including ox hair for plasterwork and cleft battens and laths for roofing and plasterwork.

**Wells Cathedral
Stonemasons**
Brunel Stoneworks
Station Road
Cheddar
Somerset
BS27 3AH

Tel: **(01934) 743544**
Fax: **(01934) 744536**

Contact:
Graham O'Hare,
Conservator

Wells Cathedral Stonemasons will supply small quantities of lime putty, from H.J.Chard and Bleaklow, and may supply some lime mortars if required. In the future they may be expanding their range of lime products.

**Woodchester
Mansion Trust**
1 The Old Town Hall
High Street
Stroud
Gloucestershire
GL5 1AP

Tel: **(01453) 750455**

Contact: Jamie Vans

Woodchester Mansion Trust is a building conservation charity which offers training courses in the repair and conservation of historic buildings. Courses include stone repair and conservation for professionals and craftsmen; practical training projects for groups of students from craft training colleges; hands-on study days for university courses in architecture and conservation; and short courses in skills such as pointing for home owners.

The Trust carries out consultancy work in building conservation, particularly in the use of lime, and can supply small quantities only of lime putty, limewash and mortars mixed to specification. An introductory booklet, *Lime Mortars,* is available by post.

**Mike Wye &
Associates**
Glebe House
Buckland Filleigh
Beaworthy
Devon
EX21 5HY

Tel: **(01409) 281644**

Makers and suppliers of traditional lime products and cob blocks, Mike Wye & Associates offer mature lime putty, lime mortars, plasters and limewash, made from the finest quality slaked Buxton lime. They hold over 100 tonnes of mature lime products in their 4500 sq. ft. warehouse for prompt delivery throughout the U.K. Lime products are supplied in sealed plastic containers, palletised if required. Lime mortars can also be supplied in 1 tonne bags.

Product	Quantity	£.p
Lime putty	25 kg tub	6.00
	30 kg tub	7.00
Lime mortar (coarse pit sand/ mature lime putty, unhaired)	40 kg tub	6.00
	1 tonne dumpy bag	100.00
Lime mortar (haired)	40 kg tub	7.00
	1 tonne dumpy bag	125.00
Lime plaster (fine pit sand/lime putty)	18 kg tub	3.70
Limewash (white)	20 litre tub	10.00
Limewash (coloured)	20 litre tub	12.00

Northern Ireland

Kilwaughter Chemical Co. Ltd.
Industrial and Agricultural Limestone Powders
Kilwaughter Limeworks
Lame
Co. Antrim
BT40 2TJ

Tel: **(01574) 260766**
Fax: **(01574) 260136**

Suppliers of lime/sand ready-mixed mortars using non-hydraulic and hydrated lime, to BS890. Dry hydrated lime can be supplied from stock. Putty and quicklime can be supplied, but are not stock items.

Product	Quantity	£.p
Hydrated lime	tonne	110.00

Narrow Water Lime Service
Newry Road
Warrenpoint
Co. Down
BT34 3LE

Tel/Fax:
(016937) 53073

Contact: Dan McPolin

Narrow Water Lime Service produces lime putty manufactured in the traditional fashion and carry out a consultancy practice, which includes site visits to advise on matters relating to the use of lime and masonry.

Workshops are given to introduce people to lime and its use in conservation and building. These include hands-on experience of slaking lime, mixing mortar, pigmenting mortar, rendering, plastering, building with stone and brick, harling and producing limewashes.

Lime putty and lime mortar are packaged in 25 kg plastic containers; limewash in 20 litre plastic containers.

Scotland

Mason's Mortar
61-67 Trafalgar Lane
Leith
Edinburgh
EH6 4DQ

Tel: **(0131) 5530503**
Fax: **(0131) 5537158**

Manufacturers of mortars for the care and repair of historic buildings, Mason's Mortar supply a wide range of lime-based products and related products and services, including high calcium lime, moderately hydraulic and eminently hydraulic types. Lime is supplied as lime putty, dry hydrate, quicklime and limewashes. Also available are coarse stuffs for all building applications, setting stuff for plastering, pre-mixed dry-bagged hydraulic lime and aggregates and lime-based mortars which have been made by slaking lime and aggregates together (hot slaked mortars), as well as grouting mixes based on lime in either a standard mix or made to order. Mason's Mortar also provide a site mixing service for hot slaked mortars and laying down lime putty in clients' pits.

The following additional related materials are supplied: HTI powder; low sulphate PFA; ground furnace slag; crushed shell and beach shells; stone dust; limestone dust and flours and aggregates; silica sands; mastic sand; brick grog (crushed brick); bentonite; powdered chalk; tallow; linseed oil (raw and boiled); goat and horse hair; riven laths (Scots pine), trisodium phosphate; formaldehyde; oxalic acid; red lead putty; red lead oxide; sepiolite; puddle clay.

Mason's tools, pointing keys, stiff bristle and limewashing brushes, gloves, goggles and dust masks; plastic and paper sacks, bolsters, chisels, and club hammers are also available.

An aggregate matching service and mortar analysis are offered to clients, along with guidance notes on using lime-based products. The firm maintains a database of suppliers of chemicals and products which may be of use to others in the conservation field and a database of sand and aggregate sources throughout the UK in order to assist contractors and specifiers in locating appropriate materials.

Prices for materials and services vary, depending on volume, and can be made available on request.

Pot Hunter
135 Comiston Road
Edinburgh
EH10 6AQ

Tel/ Fax:
(0131) 4475660
Fax: **(0131) 3135302**

Contact:
James McCormack

Pot Hunter supply special products and services for the repair and conservation of historic buildings, including St. Astier Pure XHN100 hydraulic lime, which is packaged in 50 kg bags.

The company's other products include brass numerals, cast brass bell pulls and fittings, cast iron railings, balconies and balusters, and other specialist items for historic buildings to exactly match originals.

Scottish Lime Centre Trust
PO Box 251
Edinburgh
EH6 4DW

Tel: **(0131) 5534999**
Fax: **(0131) 5537158**

Contact:
the Technical Manager

The Scottish Lime Centre Trust offers specialist advice and assistance to building owners, professionals and contractors, including training workshops, building evaluations, analyses of surviving mortars and job-specific recommendations and specifications. Supply of traditional lime-based materials is linked to this service and pre-mixed mortars are specified to provide compatible matching mortars for individual jobs. Mortars are made up either from quicklime and sand or from matured lime putty and sand as appropriate, using sands selected from the Centre's extensive database of Scottish aggregates. A range of limewashes is available from stock, and special limewashes can be made up to order.

Enquiries about imported hydraulic limes are also welcome. Jurakalk natural eminently hydraulic lime from Switzerland and St. Astier natural hydraulic lime from France are generally available from stock. The Centre can also supply specialist tools and other materials to order.

Product	Quantity	£.p
Ready-mixed lime mortars	40 kg	p.o.a.
High calcium lime putty	35 kg	p.o.a.
Feebly hydraulic lime putty	35 kg	p.o.a.
High calcium quicklime	30 kg	p.o.a.
Jurakalk	40 kg	p.o.a.
St. Astier	50 kg	p.o.a.
Goat hair	kg	p.o.a.
Limewash (white)	20 litre	p.o.a.
Limewash (standard colours)	20 litre	p.o.a.
Limewash (special colours)	20 litre	p.o.a.
Tallow limewash	20 litre	p.o.a.

Sieved limewashes 10% extra.

Wales

Bryn Gilby
17 Heol Mair
Litchard
Bridgend
Mid Glamorgan

Tel: **(01656) 659040**
Mobile: **(0850) 047714**

Bryn Gilby manufactures lime putty and supplies lime/sand mortars, haired lime/sand plaster and limewash (with or without tallow and pigments) to order.

Prices for lime putty and limewash (white or pigmented) are available on application.

Ty-Mawr Lime
Ty-Mawr Farm
Llangasty
Brecon
Powys
LD3 7PJ

Tel: **(01874) 658249**
Fax: **(01874) 658567**

Ty-Mawr Lime is a family-run business in the Brecon Beacons National Park producing lime-based products and supplying other traditional building materials and tools. All Ty-Mawr lime is slaked on site, then left to mature for at least three months. Hot-lime mortar is produced using the traditional method of slaking the lime with the moisture from the aggregate through mixing, which gives a good bond between the lime and the aggregate. Hot-mix mortars are all produced in a mortar mill specifically designed to ensure a thorough mix. Ty-Mawr produce a standard hot mix suitable for general building work or can tailor mixes to match an analysis result.

The company aim to support the healthy resurgence in using traditional materials in the repair and conservation of old buildings by ensuring the production and supply of high quality products at competitive prices. Analysis, specification service, advice and training courses are also offered.

Republic of Ireland

Robert Butcher & Son
Ivy Farm
Kereight
Ballyhoge
Enniscorthy
Co. Wexford

Tel: **353 (0) 54 47615**

Contact: Robert Butcher

Robert Butcher & Son act as building and paint consultants for historic and traditional buildings. They helped Clogrennane Lime to develop White Rhino lime putty, and can source traditional materials, including lime putty, throughout Ireland. UK office in Crockerton, tel: (01985) 846990.

Clogrennane Lime
Co. Ltd.
Carlow
Co. Carlow
Republic of Ireland

Tel: **353 (0) 503 31811**
Fax: **353 (0) 503 31607**

Clogrennane Lime have been extracting high quality calcium limestone from their quarry on-site since 1816. Most of the limestone is burned to form quicklime and this is supplied to customers in three different grades. The company supply lime putty and lime mortars for restoration and decoration projects, and dry hydrated lime in bags or bulk tankers is also available.

The company use the White Rhino trade name for all their lime products. Their entire range of products is available in the UK through their agent, Potmolen Paint in Warminster.

Product	Quantity	£.p
Quicklime	tonne	60.00
Hydrated lime	25 kg bag	2.00
Lime putty	25 kg tub	8.00

Chapter 3

Glossary

Agricultural lime
Crushed limestone (mainly calcium carbonate) which is used to neutralise soil acidity and improve crop production. The very limited solubility of solid calcium carbonate means that the chalk or other limestone needs to be in powdered form, and the traditional practice was to use lime produced in kilns. Today, however, limestone can be crushed and powdered economically and does not require burning. Since unburnt calcium carbonate ($CaCO_3$) will not act as a binder in mortars, 'agricultural limes' should be avoided for building use.

Air-lime
Another term for non-hydraulic lime, which hardens with exposure to carbon dioxide in air (as opposed to hydraulic lime, which hardens by chemical reaction with water). This is a translation of a term used in most European countries.

Air slaking
The result of excessive exposure of quicklime to air. The quicklime will absorb moisture from the air, forming hydroxides and carbonates in an uncontrolled way.

Argillaceous limestone
Limestone which contains a considerable quantity of clay or shale in addition to calcium and magnesium carbonates. It is burned to produce hydraulic lime.

Available lime
(Also known as free lime.) The total calcium oxide (CaO) and/or calcium hydroxide ($Ca(OH)_2$) content in a quicklime or hydrate.

Blue lias
English limestone of the lias formation of the Jurassic system, burned to produce hydraulic lime. Outcrops of this distinctive blue-coloured stone occur on the North Somerset and South Wales coasts.

Chalk
Soft, fine-grained, fossiliferous form of calcium carbonate, of varying

colour and purity. White chalk may be extremely pure (98-99% calcium carbonate), whereas grey chalks may contain up to 20% of impurities.

Coarse stuff
A mixture of slaked lime putty and sand/aggregate which is stored, protected from air, for as long as possible before being used as a base for lime mortar and render.

Dolomitic lime
See Magnesian lime.

Dolomitic limestone
Limestone that contains a large proportion of magnesium carbonate, in addition to calcium carbonate. Pure dolomitic stone contains a ratio of 40-44% $MgCO_3$ to 54-58% $CaCO_3$. However, the term is more loosely applied to any carbonate rock containing magnesium carbonate. In the UK, the term 'magnesian limestone' is preferred to 'dolomitic limestone', since UK sources of magnesian limestone have a relatively low magnesium carbonate content. Dolomitic/magnesian limestones are not currently burned for lime in the UK, although they are used in the United States. The American classification of magnesian or dolomitic limestones is determined by the amount of magnesium carbonate as follows:

High calcium limestone	0.5% magnesium carbonate content
Magnesian limestone	5-35% magnesium carbonate content
Dolomitic limestone	35-45% magnesium carbonate content

Fat lime
(Also known as pure, white or rich lime.) Lime which contains approximately 5% or less of impurities such as silica and alumina, as distinct from an impure or hydraulic lime. It slakes rapidly, producing much heat and expanding by two to three times its initial volume. It should be noted that 'fat lime' is a traditional term, which does not conform to the most recent relevant lime standard, European Prestandard ENV 459-1: 1995.

Free lime
See Available lime.

Hard-burned lime
Quicklime that has been calcined or burned at high temperature and is consequently of high density and moderate to low chemical reactivity.

Hydrated lime

Dry powder obtained by hydrating quicklime with enough water to combine chemically to form hydroxides. Hydrated limes may be high calcium limes (consisting mainly of calcium hydroxide) or hydraulic limes (containing calcium hydroxide in addition to calcium silicates and aluminates). In the UK, the term 'hydrated lime' is most commonly used to refer to a dry powder of non-hydraulic lime (calcium hydroxide).

Hydraulic lime

A form of lime with hydraulic properties of varying degrees, which can set and harden under water. Hydraulic limes set by chemical reaction with water (as opposed to non-hydraulic limes, which harden by reaction with carbon dioxide in the air).

Hydraulic limes contain varying amounts of calcium silicates, calcium aluminates and calcium hydroxide produced either by the burning of argillaceous limestones or (in continental European countries) by the addition of various hydraulic materials. In the European Prestandard ENV 459-1: 1995, hydraulic limes produced from argillaceous limestones are designated NHL (Natural Hydraulic Limes), while limes modified by the addition of 'suitable pozzolanic or hydraulic materials, up to 20% by mass' are designated NHL-P. This standard also notes that in some countries masonry cements conforming to ENV 413-1 'Masonry Cement – Part 1: Specification' with less than 3% available lime may be termed *chaux hydrauliques artificielles* (artificial hydraulic limes) or *calce eminentamente idraulica artificiale* (artificial eminently hydraulic lime).

Hydraulic limes have traditionally been classified according to the percentage of silica and alumina present, as follows:

Feebly hydraulic lime	less than 12% silica and alumina content
Moderately hydraulic lime	12-18% silica and alumina content
Eminently or very hydraulic lime	18-25% silica and alumina content

Lean lime

(Also known as poor lime.) Lime which contains more than 5% of impurities and is therefore less pure than fat lime. Lean lime slakes more slowly than fat lime, with a smaller increase in volume. It is less plastic than fat lime and can be white or off-white in colour.

Limestone

General term for all sedimentary rocks whose principal constituent is calcium carbonate.

Limewash

A traditional surface finish consisting, in its most basic form, of slaked lime and water. However, materials such as tallow, casein or linseed oil are often added to create a more durable and water-resistant treatment (particularly for external use). Similarly, appropriate pigments may be added for colour.

Lime putty

A form of lime hydrate in a wet, plastic putty consistency, containing free water.

Lump lime

See Quicklime.

Magnesian lime

(Also known as dolomitic lime.) Lime which contains 10-20% (or more) of magnesium oxide. Such limes are produced by burning dolomitic or magnesian limestones, which contain a considerable amount of magnesium carbonate in addition to calcium carbonate (see Dolomitic limestone). Magnesian limes have similar properties to calcium limes, although they slake much more slowly. Magnesian limes for building are not currently produced or supplied in the UK.

Magnesian limestone

Limestone which contains more magnesium carbonate than high calcium stone but less than dolomite. Authorities are not in full agreement as to its range of magnesium carbonate, but the consensus favours 5-35% (see also Dolomitic limestone).

Natural ('Roman') cements

A class of hydraulic materials between eminently hydraulic limes and modern artificial cements. They are produced by burning argillaceous limestones like septaria which have an extremely high clay content (30-50%) as well as some iron oxide. Unlike hydraulic limes, calcined natural cements cannot slake in lump form and must be ground before use. They will set very rapidly under water (in 15 minutes to one hour) and can attain quite high strengths.

Natural cements were developed at the end of the eighteenth century and were once produced at a number of locations in the UK. However, there is no longer any domestic production and all such materials are now imported.

Non-hydraulic lime

(Also known as air-lime.) Lime which will not set by chemical reaction with water but requires exposure to carbon dioxide in the air in order to harden.

Poor lime

See Lean lime.

Pure lime

See Fat lime.

Quicklime

(Also known as lump lime.) A lime oxide (mainly calcium oxide (CaO) in a high-calcium lime) produced by calcining or burning limestone so that carbon dioxide is liberated. It must be slaked with water to form calcium hydroxide before use.

Rich lime

See Fat lime.

Slaked lime

A hydrated form of non-hydraulic lime which may be a dry powder or a putty. In practice, slaked lime is obtained by adding quicklime to water.

Soft-burned lime

Quicklime that has been calcined at a relatively low temperature and which is characterised by high porosity and chemical reactivity.

White lime

See Fat lime.

Chapter 4

Bibliography and Standards

Books and Scientific Reports

Ashurst, J. Mortars, *Plasters and Renders in Conservation.* Ecclesiastical Architects and Surveyors Association (EASA), 2nd edition, 1996 (in press).

Ashurst, J. and Ashurst, N. *Practical Building Conservation* Vol. 2: Terracotta, Brick and Earth. English Heritage Technical Handbook, Gower Technical Press, Aldershot, 1988.

Ashurst, J. and Ashurst, N. *Practical Building Conservation* Vol. 3: Mortars, Plasters and Renders. English Heritage Technical Handbook, Gower Technical Press, Aldershot, 1988.

Boynton, R.S. *The Chemistry and Technology of Lime and Limestone.* 2nd edition, John Wiley & Sons, New York, 1980.

Brereton, C. *The Repair of Historic Buildings: Advice on Principles and Methods.* 2nd edition, English Heritage, London, 1995.

Bristow, I. *Interior House-Painting Colours and Technology 1615-1840.* Yale University Press, New Haven and London, 1996.

Cowper, A.D. *Building Research Special Report No. 9: Lime and Lime Mortars.* HMSO, London, 1927.

Davey, N. *A History of Building Materials.* Phoenix House, London, 1961, pp. 121–127.

Eckel, E.C. *Cements, Limes and Plaster.* John Wiley & Sons, New York, 1928.

Hill, N., Holmes, S., Mather, D. eds. *Lime and Other Alternative Cements.* Intermediate Technology Publications, London, 1992.

Lea, F.M. *The Chemistry of Cement and Concrete.* 3rd edition, Arnold Ltd., London, 1988, pp. 415–453.

Powys, A.R. *Repair of Ancient Buildings.* 3rd edition, SPAB, London, 1995 (first published 1929).

Schofield, Jane. *Lime in Building: A Practical Guide.* Revised 2nd edition. Cullompton Press, 1995.

Teutonico, J. M., McCaig, I., Burns, C. and Ashurst, J. 'The Smeaton Project: Factors Affecting the Properties of Lime-Based Mortars'. *Bulletin of the Association for Preservation Technology,* Vol. 25, Nos. 3-4 (September 1994), pp. 32–49.

Torraca, G. *Porous Building Materials: Materials Science for Architectural Conservation.* ICCROM, Rome, 1988.

Vicat, L.J. *A Practical and Scientific Treatise on Calcareous Mortars and Cements, Artificial and Natural.* 1928, translated by Capt. J.T. Smith, John Weale, London, 1987.

Williams, Richard. *Limekilns and Limeburning.* Shire Publications Ltd., Aylesbury, 1989.

Wingate, M. *Small–Scale Lime Burning.* Intermediate Technology Publications, London, 1995.

Guidelines and Other Information

Building Limes Forum
2 Cross Cottage
Kiddington
Nr. Woodstock
Oxfordshire
OX20 1BN

The Building Limes Forum publishes a bi-annual journal, *Lime News,* which contains reports, papers, reprints, letters and other information related to the historical and current use of building limes. Enquiries regarding membership of the Forum (which includes a subscription to *Lime News*) should be directed to the address above.

Building Research Establishment
Address for publications:
Construction Research Communications Ltd.
151 Rosebury Avenue
London
EC1R 4QX

Tel: **(0171) 5056622**
Fax: **(0171) 5056606**

DAS 70: *External Masonry Walls: Eroding Mortars – Repoint or Rebuild?*
Digest 177: *Decay and Conservation of Stone Masonry.*
Digest 196: *External Rendered Finishes.*
Digest 362: *Building Mortar.*

Historic Scotland
Technical Conservation, Research and Education Division
Publications Section
Scottish Conservation Bureau
Longmore House
Salisbury Place
Edinburgh
EH9 1SH

Tel: **(0131) 6688606**
Fax: **(0131) 6688869**

Technical Advice Note No. 1: *Preparation and Use of Lime Mortars.*
Technical Advice Note No. 2: *Conservation of Plasterwork.*

Intermediate Technology Development Group
Intermediate Technology Publications
103/105 Southampton Row
London
WC1B 4HH

Hydraulic Lime: An Introduction (pamphlet in series on low-cost cements).

The Society for the Protection of Ancient Buildings
37 Spital Square
London
E1 6DY

Tel: **(0171) 3771644**
Fax: **(0171) 2475296**

SPAB Information Sheet No. 1: *Basic Limewash.*
SPAB Information Sheet No. 4: *The Need for Old Buildings to 'Breathe'.*
SPAB Information Sheet No. 9: *An Introduction to Building Limes.*
SPAB Technical Pamphlet No. 5: *Pointing Stone and Brick Walling.*

Standards

British Standards Institution
389 Chiswick High Road
London W4 4AL

Tel: **(0181) 9969000**
Fax: **(0181) 9967400**

BS 890: 1995. *Specification for Building Limes.*

BS ENV 459–1: 1995.
Building Lime. Part 1. Definitions, Specifications and Conformity Criteria
(European Prestandard).

BS EN 459–2: 1995. *Building Lime.* Part 2. Test Methods.

BS 6463–1: 1984.
Quicklime, Hydrated Lime and Natural Calcium Carbonate. Part 1.
Methods of Sampling.

BS 6463–2: 1984.
Quicklime, Hydrated Lime and Natural Calcium Carbonate. Part 2.
Methods of Chemical Analysis.

BS 6463–3: 1987.
Quicklime, Hydrated Lime and Natural Calcium Carbonate. Part 3.
Methods of Test for Physical Properties of Quicklime.

BS 6463–4: 1987.
Quicklime, Hydrated Lime and Natural Calcium Carbonate. Part 4.
Methods of Test for Physical Properties of Hydrated Lime and Lime Putty.

BS 6100–6.1: 1984.
British Standard Glossary of Building and Civil Engineering Terms. Part 6:
Concrete and Plaster, section 6.1 Binders.

BS 4721: 1981 (1986). *Specification for Ready-mixed Building Mortars.*

BS 4551: 1980. *Methods of Testing Mortars, Screeds and Plasters.*

BS 1199 and 1200: 1976.
Specifications for Building Sands from Natural Sources.

BS 5262: 1991. *Code of Practice for External Renderings.*

BS 5390: 1976 (1984). *Code of Practice for Stone Masonry.*

BS 6270–1: 1982.
Code of Practice for Cleaning and Surface Repair of Buildings. Part 1:
Natural Stone, Cast Stone and Clay and Calcium Silicate Brick Masonry.
Currently under revision.

Chapter 5

Suppliers by Region

Anglia

(Essex, Cambridgeshire, Lincolnshire, Norfolk, Suffolk)

Arnold & Gould
Ashfield Traditional
Hendry & Sons Ltd.
Hirst Conservation Materials Ltd.
Mascot Traditional Materials
Textured European Finishes

Midlands

(Bedfordshire, Buckinghamshire, Derbyshire, Hereford & Worcester, Hertfordshire, Leicestershire, Northamptonshire, Nottinghamshire, Shropshire, Staffordshire, Warwickshire, West Midlands,)

Bleaklow Industries Ltd.
Buxton Lime Industries Ltd.
Cy-Pres
Lawrence Long Ltd.
RMC Industrial Minerals Ltd.
Telling Lime Products

North

(Cheshire, Cleveland, Cumbria, Durham, Humberside, Lancashire, Greater Manchester, Merseyside, Northumberland, Tyne & Wear, North Yorkshire, South Yorkshire, West Yorkshire)

Building Conservation Services
W. Fein and Sons Ltd.
Optiroc Ltd.
The Real Paint & Varnish Company
Elaine Rigby and Charles Blackett-Ord
Singleton Birch Ltd.
Tilcon Ltd.

South East
(Hampshire, Greater London, Kent, Surrey, East Sussex, West Sussex)

Bursledon Brickworks

Cathedral Works Organisation (Chichester) Ltd.

Dolmen

The Lime Centre

J. Negus

Papers and Paints Ltd.

Weald & Downland Open Air Museum

South West
(Avon, Berkshire, Cornwall, Devon, Dorset, Gloucestershire, Oxfordshire, Somerset, Wiltshire)

ARC Southern

Blue Circle Industries Plc

H. J. Chard & Sons

Cornish Lime Company

Farrow & Ball Ltd.

A. E. Griffin & Son

Hydraulic Lias Limes Ltd.

I.J.P. Building Conservation

Liz Induni

J. Layzell & Sons

Limebase Products Ltd.

Potmolen Lime

Potmolen Paint

Rose of Jericho

Severn Valley Stone Co.

J. & J. Sharpe

Shillingstone Lime & Stone Co. Ltd.

Speedlime

Tamar Trading Co. Ltd.

TEC Build Supplies Ltd.

The Traditional Lime Co.

Twyford Lime Products

Wells Cathedral Stonemasons

Woodchester Mansion Trust

Mike Wye & Associates

Northern Ireland

Kilwaughter Chemical Co. Ltd.

Narrow Water Lime Service

Scotland

Mason's Mortar

Pot Hunter

Scottish Lime Centre Trust

Wales

Bryn Gilby

Ty-Mawr Lime

Republic of Ireland

Robert Butcher & Son

Clogrennane Lime Co. Ltd.

Product Finder

Producers and Suppliers

Producers and Suppliers	Page number	Quicklime	Non-hydraulic lime (hydrate)	Non-hydraulic lime (putty)	Hydraulic lime	Lime/sand mortars	Limewashes	Pigments	Brickdust and HTI powder	Plaster/render mixes	Lime-based paints	Tallow (oils)	Laths	Hair
ARC Southern	12	●			●									
Arnold & Gould	12													●
Ashfield Traditional	12					●	●							●
Bleaklow Industries Ltd.	13		●		●	●								
Blue Circle Industries Plc	13		●											
Building Conservation Services	13		●		●				●	●		●	●	
Bursledon Brickworks	14		●	●	●	●	●		●			●	●	
Robert Butcher & Son	41	●	●	●		●								
Buxton Lime Industries Ltd.	15	●	●	●						●				
Cathedral Works Organisation (Chichester) Ltd.	15			●	●				●					
H. J. Chard & Sons	16	●	●	●	●			●	●	●		●	●	●
Clogrennane Lime Co. Ltd.	41	●	●	●		●								
Cornish Lime Company	17	●		●	●	●	●	●	●	●	●	●	●	●
Cy-Pres	17			●		●	●		●	●		●		
Dolmen	18			●	●	●	●	●	●	●		●	●	●
Farrow & Ball Ltd.	18					●								
W. Fein & Sons Ltd.	19													●
Bryn Gilby	40			●		●	●	●						
A. E. Griffin & Son	19			●				●	●		●			
Hendry & Sons Ltd.	19		●	●		●	●	●		●		●	●	●
Hirst Conservation Materials Ltd.	20	●	●	●	●	●	●	●	●	●	●			●
Hydraulic Lias Limes Ltd.	21		●	●	●	●								
I.J.P. Building Conservation	21			●		●	●	●		●			●	●
Liz Induni	22						●	●			●			
Kilwaughter Chemical Co. Ltd.	37		●			●	●	●		●				
J. Layzell & Sons	22	●	●	●	●	●	●	●	●	●		●	●	●
The Lime Centre	23	●		●	●	●	●	●	●	●		●	●	●
Limebase Products Ltd.	23	●		●		●	●	●	●	●		●	●	
Lawrence Long Ltd.	24													●
Mascot Traditional Materials	24		●	●	●	●	●		●	●	●	●		●
Mason's Mortar	38	●	●	●	●	●	●	●	●	●	●	●	●	●

Producers and Suppliers	Page number	Quicklime	Non-hydraulic lime (hydrate)	Non-hydraulic lime (putty)	Hydraulic lime	Lime/sand mortars	Limewashes	Pigments	Brickdust and HTI powder	Plaster/render mixes	Lime-based paints	Tallow (oils)	Laths	Hair
Narrow Water Lime Service	37		●		●	●								
J. Negus	24		●		●									
Optiroc	25	●	●	●	●	●	●	●	●	●	●	●		●
Papers & Paints Ltd.	25		●					●			●	●		
Pot Hunter	39			●										
Potmolen Lime	25					●			●					
Potmolen Paint	26		●	●			●	●		●	●			●
The Real Paint & Varnish Co.	26		●		●	●	●			●	●	●		
E. Rigby & C. Blackett-Ord	27	●	●				●							●
RMC Industrial Minerals Ltd.	27	●	●											
Rose of Jericho	28		●		●	●			●	●	●			
Scottish Lime Centre Trust	39	●	●	●	●	●	●	●	●		●		●	●
Severn Valley Stone Co.	29	●		●	●	●	●	●	●		●		●	●
J. & J. Sharpe	29	●	●	●	●	●	●	●	●		●			●
Shillingstone Lime & Stone Co. Ltd.	30	●	●	●	●									
Singleton Birch Ltd.	30	●	●	●										
Speedlime	31			●										
Tamar Trading Co. Ltd.	31	●	●	●	●	●	●	●	●			●	●	●
TEC Build Supplies Ltd	31				●	●			●					
Telling Lime Products	32				●	●	●		●	●				
Textured European Finishes	32					●	●		●	●				
Tilcon Ltd.	33		●		●				●					
The Traditional Lime Co.	33			●	●	●	●		●					
Twyford Lime Products	34			●	●	●			●					
Ty-Mawr Lime	40	●	●	●	●	●	●	●	●	●	●	●	●	●
Weald & Downland Open Air Museum	34												●	●
Wells Cathedral Stonemasons	35	●	●	●	●	●	●	●	●	●				
Woodchester Mansion Trust	35			●	●	●								
Mike Wye & Associates	35	●		●		●	●	●	●	●	●	●		●

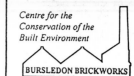

DONHEAD
PUBLISHING

Books for Conservation Professionals

❖ Practical Stone Masonry
P R Hill and J C E David

This book covers the basic methods of working stone, the making of specialized tools, and, for the first time, a full analysis of the procedures for setting-out for repairs. A broad description of the nature and problems of stone also includes guidance on selection. In addition, it looks at the causes of decay in stone and outline methods for repair of both stone and mortar.

1995   288 pages   Hardback   1 873394 14 4   £32.00

❖ Processes of Urban Stone Decay
Proceedings of SWAPNET '95 Stone Weathering Conference held in Belfast, 19–20 May 1995.
Edited by B.J. Smith and P.A. Warke

This volume offers a multi-disciplinary approach to the study of decay processes. It shows the range of current work and the possibilities for alternative approaches to problem solving. The book begins with an overview of some of the theoretical issues, looks at the processes of stone decay, and then reviews the methods used in the analysis of stone durability and weathering response to environmental conditions. It concludes with some specific examples of research and conservation practice.

1996   288 pages   Hardback   1 873394 20 9   £35.00

❖ Cleaning Historic Buildings
Nicola Ashurst

This comprehensive guide, offers essential practical advice on appropriate cleaning techniques supported by valuable case study material and photographs. Current cleaning practices are examined along with the role and need for analysis of substrates and soiling. It suggests methods for dealing with special cleaning problems and provides an assessment of the cleaning methods currently available.

Volume 1: 1994 Hb 1 873394 01 2 264 pages £32.00
Volume 2: 1994 Hb 1 873394 11 X 272 pages £32.00
Volumes 1 & 2 (set price) 1 873394 12 8   £58.00

❖ Stone Cleaning
and the nature, soiling and decay mechanisms of stone.
Proceedings of the International Conference held in Edinburgh UK 14-16 April 1992. **Edited by Robin G M Webster**

Contributions examine the problems and reasons for building soiling, along with advantages and disadvantages of chemical and wet/dry abrasive cleaning methods. They document the results of recent laboratory experiments with valuable case studies featuring examples of the cleaning of architectural stonework.

1992   320 pages   Hardback   1 873394 09 8   £32.00

Donhead Publishing Ltd, Lower Coombe, Donhead St Mary, Shaftesbury, Dorset SP7 9LY. Tel: 01747 828422 Fax: 01747 828522

Reply Form

Although every effort has been made to ensure that the information given in this directory is correct, mistakes may occur and circumstances may have changed since going to press. English Heritage would be grateful if readers would make any errors or omissions known to them so that the information contained in this directory can be updated in future editions. Please use this form to send us your comments and suggestions.

Your name

Your address

Your telephone No.

Your fax No.

To revise a listing or include a new supplier

Name of Company

Address of Company

Tel. No.

Fax No.

Person to contact

Brief (Maximum 100 words) description of company and services offered

Please list the products offered by the company

Product	Quantity	£.p

Do you have any comments or suggestions that would help us to improve this directory in future editions? If so, please write them here:

May we contact you to discuss these proposals in more detail? Yes/No

Signature   Date

Please return this form to:
Lime Directory Editor
Architectural Conservation Team
English Heritage
23 Savile Row
London
W1X 1AB